REAL SCIENCE, REAL FAITH

Colin Russell, Professor Emeritus of the History of Science and Technology, The Open University

Martin H.P. Bott, Professor Emeritus of Geophysics, Durham University

Roy Peacock, Visiting Professor of Aerospace Science, University of Pisa

Sir John T. Houghton, CBE, Chairman of the Royal Commission on Environmental Pollution

Ghillean T. Prance, FRS, Director of the Royal Botanic Gardens, Kew

Sir Robert L.F. Boyd, FRS, CBE, Chairman of London Bible College and Professor Emeritus of Physics, University College, London

Andrew Miller, Principal and Vice-Chancellor Stirling University and Professor Emeritus of Biochemistry, Edinburgh University

Duncan W. Vere, Professor Emeritus of Therapeutics, University of London

Colin J. Humphreys, Goldsmiths' Professor of Materials Science, University of Cambridge

Elizabeth Rhodes, formerly Lecturer in Chemical Engineering, University College, Swansea

Roger G. Bolton, Head of Regulatory Affairs Group, Zeneca

Malcolm A. Jeeves, CBE, Honorary Research Professor of Psychology, St Andrews University

Montagu G. Barker, formerly Consultant Psychiatrist and Clinical Lecturer, University of Bristol

Ray Gambell, OBE, Secretary, International Whaling Commission

R.J. (Sam) Berry, Professor of Genetics, University College, London and Member, General Synod of the Church of England

Donald M. MacKay, formerly Granada Professor of Communication, Keeley University

Christians in Science is a professional Christian group which has existed, under various names, since 1943. Membership is open to all Christians with a scientific training or a professional interest in science: scientists working in research and development, school students and undergraduates working towards science degrees, science lecturers, teachers and administrators, science writers, philosophers, theologians and others who have an active interest in the relationship between science and religious belief. Further information is available from Christians in Science, Atholl Centre, Atholl Road, Pitlochry, Perthshire PH16 5BX.

Real Science, Real Faith

Edited by
PROFESSOR R.J. BERRY

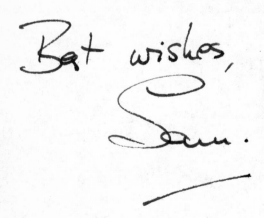

Best wishes,

Sam.

CHRISTIANS IN SCIENCE

MONARCH
Crowborough

First published 1991
Reprinted 1995

British Library Cataloguing in Publication Data

Berry, R.J.
  Real science, real faith.
  1. Religion. Related to science
  I. Title
  215

ISBN 1–85424–125–7

Produced by Bookprint Creative Services
P.O. Box 827, BN21 3YJ, England for
MONARCH PUBLICATIONS
Broadway House, The Broadway
Crowborough, East Sussex TN6 1HQ.
Printed in Great Britain

Contents

Foreword

I am not scientifically trained—unless we can still boast that theology is the queen of the sciences—but I am made constantly aware that we are living in a scientific and technological age. It is therefore all the more vital to understand that real science and real faith can live happily together. These personal testimonies demonstrate that this agreement is not always easily found. Here are honest accounts of wrestling to faith and in faith from people with scientific education and expertise. These essays remind us that as Christians we never have to anaesthetise our mind. Indeed Scripture calls us constantly to use our minds. All must be under the sovereign authority of Scripture and we need constantly to exercise intellectual humility. It is fatal to disengage our mind in our Christian pilgrimage.

This book will be a tremendous help and encouragement to scientists who may be going through a struggle in their pilgrimage. It will confirm faith but in a totally honest way. It is equally prescribed reading for non-scientists who do need to understand the tensions that can arise and the process through which faith is strengthened in the mind and life of Christians who are scientists. There is not absolute agreement between all the essays in this book but there is the basic unanimity of belief in the lordship of Christ, the authority of God's word and the validity of personal Christian experience. Reading these chapters will help us to understand those who are Christians and scientists and to pray for them. May there be more convinced Christians in this important area of life and may we all learn the rich variety of God's dealings with his children.

Philip Hacking
Chairman, The Keswick Convention

Introduction

This book is the story of fifteen men and one woman. They are all professional scientists who have achieved success in their careers and they are all committed Christians. There the resemblance between them ends. Every one received the same invitation: to write about his or her faith, and how this affects and is affected by the practice of science. The result will make anyone who believes all scientists are monochrome automata think again. Further, anyone who assumes that it is only possible for a scientist to be a Christian if his science and faith are kept separate must also think again. The warfare between science and Christianity is a historical myth, as Colin Russell, one of the most distinguished British historians of science, points out in Chapter 1.

The fifteen chapters that follow are written by people who have 'made it' in their chosen careers. However, the reason for commissioning the particular group of contributors was not to add one more book of Christian success stories, but simply to demonstrate that Christians can rise to the top of the scientific tree without in any way compromising their allegiance to Christ. Several of the authors describe how God has called them to be scientists, and given them opportunities because they were in God's place in God's time. If there is a spiritual lesson to learn from reading the testimonies herein, it is that of obedience, not of automatic blessing on the chosen few.

And do not be side-tracked by the notion that obedience

comes easily to those that God favours. We read in the following pages of sickness, indecision, and disappointment, as well as answered prayer and worldly honours. All of us must come as sinners before the cross of Christ if we are ever to be of use to him. But there is no one way to do this. In this book are stories of those brought up in Christian homes, of those who found faith at a time of crisis, of those who came to the Lord over a period of years, and of those who experienced a relatively sudden conversion. There is probably no difference between the experiences of our fifteen scientists and any random group of Christians; there is no bypass to heaven for the privileged.

Some of the scientists in this book have written mainly of their science and its implications for faith (notably Andrew Miller, Malcolm Jeeves and Monty Barker); others have written more of their own pilgrimage (particularly Roy Peacock, Elizabeth Rhodes and Ghillean Prance). This demonstrates the individuality of the contributors, but it also brings a range of perspectives on the faith-science interface. The ultimate problem all of us have to face relates to the activity of God in this world. A God who has no control over events, who cannot answer prayer or affect our lives, is hardly worth believing in. Paul wrote that if the Christian God was like that 'our preaching is useless, and so is your faith' (1 Cor 15:14). But the message that comes over loud and clear from all fifteen scientists is that our faith is *not* 'useless', that God *has* intervened in the world he made, and that 'in him all things hold together' (Col 1:17).

The result is not a textbook of apologetics, but all the classical science-faith problems are touched on—miracles, determinancy, 'natural laws', answered prayer, healing, and so on. The traditional bogey of evolution or creation is referred to by two-thirds of the writers, all of them making the point that there is no necessary conflict between the two. Indeed, the creation controversy is an excellent example of the commonest false assumption about God:

the assumption that if we know the 'cause' behind an event we know everything about that event and can exclude God from it. This was answered at least as long ago as Aristotle, who distinguished different sorts of causation (especially 'formal' and 'material'). For example, it is possible to describe a painting entirely in terms of the distribution of chemicals that make it up, or entirely in terms of the design of its artist. Both descriptions refer to the same physical object and both are wholly true, but either by itself is incomplete as an explanation of the painting. It is possible to think of God's action in the world in exactly the same way: knowing *how* something comes to pass does not mean that we know *why* it does. In general terms, the scientist is concerned with answering 'how' questions, while the Bible and revelation are concerned with 'why' questions. Indeed, science cannot deal with 'why' questions; they are un-approachable by its methodology. This does not mean they are improper; but we cannot expect to find answers to them from science.

The distinction between 'how' and 'why' questions is at the heart of the comment by the astronomer Johannes Kepler that, in his scientific work, he was 'thinking God's thoughts after him'. In terms of evolution, we can get a scientific understanding of the mechanisms by which the earth and its life have come to be as we know them today, but it is beyond science to tell us *why* the world and humankind is as it is. The writer to the Hebrews is explicit that it is '*by faith* we understand that the universe was formed at God's command' (Heb 11:3, italics added).

The complementarity of scientific and divine (or meta-physical) accounts of God's activity was an emphasis of the late Donald MacKay, engineer turned brain investigator and philosopher, one of the most incisive science-faith explorers of recent generations. Some of our fifteen scientists (notably Robert Boyd and Duncan Vere) pay tribute to the help they received from Donald Mackay, and it has seemed appropriate to include in this volume a sixteenth contribution, a previously published essay by Professor MacKay. This sixteenth chapter is the only one not written specifically for this book; it was originally published as a small booklet in 1960, and is not a testimony as such. But it does summarise many of the issues raised in the other chapters, and is a positive contribution to 'real science, real faith'. It seems an appropriate way to conclude this symposium.

Surprised by Science

Colin Russell – Chemist and historian of science

Professor Colin A. Russell, BSc, MSc, PhD, DSc, FRSC.
Born 1928. Educated Epsom Grammar School, University
College, Hull, and University College, London.
Professor Emeritus of the History of Science and Technology,
the Open University.
President, British Society for the History of Science,
1986–88.
Member, National Railway Museum Advisory Committee.
Dexter Award, American Chemical Society, 1990.
President, Christians in Science since 1988.
Vice-President, Universities and Colleges Christian
Fellowship since 1987.

Two discoveries

Life is full of surprises; things rarely turn out as one
expects. My own commitment to science was like that. At
school I actually enjoyed languages more than science for
several years. Perhaps the fact that I started Latin as early
as the age of nine had something to do with it. What I
did not know then was that the way we were taught Latin
had much in common with the methods of science. We
mainly learned grammar, grinding out declensions and

conjugations, and memorising rules such as gerundive attraction and the ablative absolute—all terribly mechanical by today's standards, yet fascinating in its own way and with a highly coherent internal logic.

Real science first came alive for me as a means to a very practical end. One winter several of us at school spent happy hours wiring up an old shed for electric lighting, about which I learned a great deal from the older boys. Electricity continued its fascination and I experimented with magnets, coils of wire and some ancient radio equipment off-loaded by a well-meaning family friend. The ultimate goal was to electrify my model railway ... but that is another story. It was self-help of an almost Victorian kind—learning from experiments, gleaning here and there from boys' books and magazines, and making many mistakes on the way. In the austere years of wartime that was all one could do.

From physics I advanced to chemistry, via the simple route of making voltaic cells (in the vain hope of being able to dispense with costly dry batteries). Rashly, my parents allowed me to purchase considerable quantities of chemicals (including concentrated mineral acids) from the local pharmacy, and a new game had begun. Chemistry now had me in its thrall. I must have been about fourteen when, lured by advertisements in *The Meccano Magazine*, I made my first solo trip to North London, to a shop selling scientific glassware. Yet another family acquaintance off-loaded a box of miscellaneous chemicals, and I soon had an assortment of lethal substances that would make the hair of today's safety officer stand on end.

Shortly after this I concluded that the best use of chemistry would be in a medical career. Sadly, this was not to be, for in those early post-war years no sixth-form biology (then an essential prerequisite for medicine) was taught in my school. So chemistry, avidly pursued as a means to that end, now seemed like being an end in itself. After I entered the sixth form I discovered two new and enduring delights. One was mathematical analysis (above all in calculus and in algebraic functions). The other was organic chemistry. With a friend who had a copy of Cohen's *Practical Organic Chemistry*, and an indulgent mother, I resorted to experiments at his home. One day we conducted the full-scale preparation of acetyl chloride in the kitchen, filling the place with hydrogen chloride vapour. Fortunately, the lady of the house was out shopping at the time. Being now thoroughly 'hooked' on science, and disregarding the well-meant advice of my headmaster to read English, I left school for university with a chemistry degree as my goal. But meanwhile something even more significant was happening.

It must have been during my later years at school that I made a discovery which seemed at the time quite independent of my interests in science. Somehow I began to realise that the Christian faith was true. I also saw that it was relevant to my condition, that it would make huge demands on me if I accepted it, and that unless I did so life would be immeasurably poorer. That is a very inadequate description of my 'discovery', for even then it was so much more than a set of rational deductions: not so much an intellectual conclusion as a personal encounter, an incredible meeting between a mere schoolboy and his Creator. This was not presumptuous arrogance. As I realised that Jesus loved *me*, and had died for *me*, there was no room for human boasting, but rather a dawning realisation of God's mercy and generosity that almost blew the mind. My conversion was not sudden, and certainly not dramatic. Gradually I recognised that Jesus was God, as he claimed to be, that I was trusting in him, and that I must therefore count myself as his disciple.

Exactly how this happened I am not sure to this day. I have had the privilege of parents and grandparents who were real Christians, with three of my great-grandfathers preachers of the gospel. To an outsider it might seem that I never stood a chance! Yet the very fact of piety at home worried and annoyed me; church-going was an unmitigated bore, and all legitimate (and not a few illegitimate) strategies were adopted to avoid religion wherever possible. For some years I was in an acute state of counter-reaction. However, as C.S. Lewis once remarked, a young agnostic cannot possibly be too careful, such is the patience, love and grace of God. Sure enough that grace eventually won me.

One day my parents heard of a group of boys meeting on Sunday afternoons on neutral territory (a local day school) and calling themselves a Crusader class. Despairing at my open rebellion against church and its organisations, they tentatively suggested that I might like to go. And so, reluctantly, I did—as a pillion passenger on a motor cycle driven at apparently breakneck speed by a young man who was one of the leaders—a young farmer later to become the Tory MP for Torridge and West Devon, Sir Peter Mills.

Here, at Epsom Crusader class, I met a lot of youngsters of my own age or above who spent an hour each week studying the Bible, singing somewhat militaristic choruses about the Christian faith to exciting and unchurchy tunes, and apparently enjoying themselves to the full. It was, I believe, through Crusaders that I entered into real faith in Jesus, and I can never be grateful enough for a movement that has led countless young men and women into the joys and challenges of Christian faith. They did so, not by manipulative or emotional exploitation, but by faithful teaching based on the Bible and by the consistent and attractive witness of lives embodying that teaching and reflecting the love of God himself.

In addition to my parents there were two people whose example was a powerful stimulus to my own faith. One, whom I encountered almost only in print, was Cecil J. Allen, Editor of a much-read monthly periodical now alas defunct: *The Crusaders' Magazine*. He happened to be also one of the most renowned railway writers of the day, and as I was an incurable railway enthusiast he already had my full attention. I had devoured his articles in secular magazines without any inkling that he was a Christian. (His autobiography, *Two Million Miles of Rail Travel*, 1965, ends with a clear Christian testimony.) He also happened to be a gifted musician and composer of some of the best tunes we used to sing.

If this were not bad enough for a young rebel, worse was to follow. Another of the Epsom leaders was a distinguished scientist and also a very good speaker at the class—Dr Jack Aitken, Reader and then Professor of Anatomy at University College, London. He had an open, honest approach to the Bible's message, and I could not help being impressed by his ability to hold to Christianity and science at one and the same time. At that point, since none of my immediate family were scientists, there was always the possibility that I could reject the faith on the grounds of science and would be in a superior position of authority if it came to an argument. Now, however, that prop was to be kicked away. This was not, of course, a *logical* verification of Christianity. Most of us, most of the time, come to the major decisions of life through a complex mixture of logical argument and intuitive deduction, with social pressures and the quirks of personal preference thrown in. This is not for one moment to deny the objective truth of the Christian gospel; just to say that in my case I must honestly admit the importance of other factors, not least the compelling testimony of these two men. So far as I am aware neither of them ever had the slightest idea that this was so.

Science in close encounter

I went up to read chemistry at University College, Hull. In the years after the war everything was extremely spartan. Accommodation for male students was in a former army transit camp, consisting largely of Nissen huts, each undivided and heated by one central coke stove. In the ferocious winter of 1946–47, kettles left on the red-hot stove at night were filled with ice next morning, and once or twice we had to dig ourselves out of snowdrifts piled against the door. It was hard enough to study under those conditions, but the difficulties were exacerbated by chronic post-war shortages of food, fuel (anyone stealing coke was to be sent down immediately), teaching accommodation, chemicals and equipment. At that time, the university took external London degrees, and the hard-pressed staff had to teach without the foggiest idea of examination content and only the sketchiest of syllabuses to guide them. (Shortly afterwards Hull received its charter as a full university and those problems were at an end.) For the first year or two student morale plummeted and fall-out rates were high; only half of those who entered the Chemistry Department in my year made it to the end and graduated.

For many students university life was not the liberating experience that it ought to be, but quite the opposite. As a relatively new Christian, my faith might have disappeared without trace had it not been for one thing: joining a handful of other Christians who incorporated themselves into a small society called the Evangelical Union—now a flourishing body at Hull and known, like its counterparts elsewhere, as a Christian Union, associated with UCCF (or IVF in my student days). Here, at the traditional meeting for freshers, I listened to a sparkling address by a young research zoologist from Cambridge—Dr Oliver Barclay, then a Travelling Secretary for IVF, later General Secretary of UCCF, and now Editor of *Science and Christian Belief*. I was jerked to my senses realising that, whatever the circumstances, we were actually *required* to witness for Christ. A subsequent remark by the speaker to the effect that we are much too concerned with our own well-being, and not enough for the glory of God, gave a further well-aimed blow at my own rueful and lugubrious reflections. For some time that lesson had to be repeatedly relearned, but I had begun to experience the grace of God in wholly new and unexpected ways. Gradually the EU grew and prospered as other students found Christ through its witness. And all the time, almost in the shadows, was another figure whose incalculable influence on generations of students can never be known in this life.

He was George Steward, Professor of Mathematics at Hull from 1930 to 1961, and an indefatigable supporter of student Christian witness through good times and bad.[1] Not only did he keep the EU together during the dark days of the war, but afterwards he often attended its functions (sitting in the back row) and, if pressed to chair a big meeting, would invariably attest his belief that science and faith went together and that, in particular, Christianity had nothing to fear at the bar of reason, but everything to gain. Such a testimony by one of the most distinguished academics in the university made a profound impression on many budding scientists, myself included. It was not then a fashionable thing to say but it had the ring of truth and, if we were already Christians, gave an edge to our studies in science.

It would, however, be misleading to suggest that a Christian faith simply made science easy. On at least two occasions the opposite was true in my experience.

One laboratory technique that we had to acquire was that of gravimetric analysis (with, I fear, little help or instruction). This involves, among other things, the precipitation, collection, purification and weighing of often minute quantities of solid material, accurate to within a fraction of a milligram. As a student I was never very good at this, and did not perfect my technique until several years later. Since we often knew what the answer ought to be, many of us would 'adjust' our experimental figures to fit. I was no exception, until one evening in my Bible reading I encountered Proverbs 11:1, 'A false balance is an abomination to the Lord'![2] Thereafter, my discipleship had to have a new dimension and I learned that, in science, as in everything else, integrity is essential. It was a long time afterwards that

I discovered something of the horrific history of scientific frauds and fakes.

The other occasion when Christian ethics impinged directly on my science was when it was suggested that I take a job in the newly formed Atomic Energy Authority. My judgement, which I now regard as immature, was that a Christian should have nothing to do with an enterprise connected, however distantly, with weapons of mass destruction. I could not then see that nuclear reactions are as much a part of God's creation as chemical change in general, and that it is what we do with them that is open to criticism. Nor did I realise the potential benefits of nuclear energy to present and future environment (nor, of course, the possibilities of a Chernobyl).

For various reasons I decided, on graduating, to become a chemistry teacher, so embarked upon a postgraduate Certificate in Education. The fact that I have never taught in a school from that day to this is just another of life's surprises. The PGCE course was not entirely wasted, however. It gave me time to catch up on general reading, to learn something of worldviews from Plato to Freud, and to write my long essay on a subject that by now was intruding a lot on my thoughts: the relationship between science and religion and, of course, its relevance to education. I never got the essay back, and have no idea what the authorities thought of it (if, indeed, it was ever marked). Nor did I bother to make a copy; if it still exists it must be buried deep in the Education Department's archives. Perhaps it is just as well.

When I left university I moved straight into higher education, and for the first half of my career taught chemistry at two colleges—at Kingston and Preston—both of which are now Polytechnics. I quite quickly specialised in organic chemistry and for ten years was in charge of that subject at Preston. It was here that I became immersed in research into heterocyclic compounds. Although the subject was new to me, to my surprise our work went well and I experienced the thrill of making and handling compound after compound that no human eye had ever seen before. I am convinced that without that kind of experience no historian, philosopher or sociologist of science can possibly empathise with the scientist and understand what really makes him or her tick. Eventually, a small research group was set up and several students obtained their doctorates in this area. My own responsibilities in the department increased, with new labs to be designed, new courses run, and plenty of other research projects in the air. My second-in-command was also a Christian, and in all this I think we were both aware of the good hand of God upon us, not because we were particularly special but because of his infinite goodness. This sense of being in the 'right place', or 'within God's will', is one of my abiding memories of those ten years of organic chemistry in Lancashire—that, and the delights of a lively and growing family.

I might have spent the rest of my life as an organic chemist had not another novel and unexpected opening arisen. For some years I had been developing an interest in history and philosophy of science, and had actually studied it part-time at University College, London, during my Kingston years. This arose from an awareness that the history of chemistry can help and enliven teaching of the science itself. I had also harboured the suspicion that the history of science bears quite strongly on certain aspects of the Christian faith (as in the evolution controversies). A new British institution called the Open University wanted someone to start the history of science and invited me to join them. In all kinds of ways it was a considerable risk, but I decided to take the post, and now our department at the OU is one of the largest in the UK.

When I started in the history of science it was often sufficient to rely on printed sources; now, however, the subject has moved to higher levels of sophistication and, as in ordinary history, manuscript evidence is crucially important. Digging into such evidence I became more certain than ever before of the mythological character of one popular belief: the idea of a more or less permanent hostility between science and religion. As trumpeted by people like Bertrand Russell, Julian Huxley, J.B.S. Haldane and others, the notion had always seemed faintly ridiculous, partly because I knew so many scientists who held the Christian faith without, it seemed, any loss of integrity, and partly because the arguments of 'scientific materialism' appeared so pathetically thin. Of course, we often see what we want to see, but here my conclusions were shared by many who certainly did not start from my position. The more I read, the more patently obvious it became that, far from being hostile to Christianity, science had owed it a great deal during the last 400 years. And many of the greatest figures in Western science had possessed not merely a conventional religious belief but a deeply-held biblical faith and personal commitment to Christ. Several graduate students of mine have multiplied illustrations of this trend.

Nor are the popular myths all about incompatability or conflict. In my inaugural lecture at the Open University I decided to challenge the notorious thesis of Lynn White that Christian convictions about dominating the earth lie at the root of our ecologic crisis.[3] Such a thesis is, I believe, undermined by detailed examination of the historical evidence. Another popular error identifies opposition to the theory of evolution with religious orthodoxy; here I owe much to a colleague in my department—Dr J.R. Moore, whose important book *The Post-Darwinian Controversies* (1979) appeared shortly after he joined the OU. His researches have unequivocally slain that particular myth (to the discomfort, it must be said, of many of my 'creationist' friends). And so I could go on.

A study of the social history of Victorian science can help to explain how this conflict-myth has been so long-running. In Britain and America the scientific communities (or part of them) felt under siege for several reasons, and one defence mechanism was to perpetrate the illusion of endemic warfare between science and Christianity, with science the inevitable victor. As I got to grips with the social history of science that fact emerged with stark clarity. Another relation between science and faith, one of symbiosis, seems much more probable, and in the rise of science in the sixteenth and seventeenth centuries we have a host of examples. Although I had long been aware of the importance of Puritanism for English science, it came home to me with great force when I had the privilege of working, on two undergraduate courses, with such different leading scholars as Reiger Hooykaas and Christopher Hill.

Seeing science in its historical context has therefore not merely failed to undermine my faith but has given it strong support. Together with the love of my wife and family it has been one of the enriching elements in life, for which I can never be too grateful. A career in science should be as truly a 'Christian vocation' as any other. After taking services in church I have occasionally been asked why I was not a clergyman. My reply, to the effect that God had called me to be a *scientist*, always evinces surprise. I often wonder why.

Notes

[1] George Coton Steward (1896–1989) was a founder member of the Research Scientists' Christian Fellowship in 1944. His obituary is in the *Bulletin* of the University of Hull, no 122 (9 February 1990): p 2, and in *Science and Christian Belief*, vol 2 (1990), p 2.

[2] There are several other passages with a similar message (Prov 16:11; 20:23; Ezek 45:10; Hos 12:7; Amos 8:5).

[3] Lynn White, 'The historical roots of our ecologic crisis', *Science* (New York), 155: 1203–1207, 1967.

Down to Earth

Martin Bott – Geologist

Professor Martin H.P. Bott, MA, PhD, FRS.
Born 1926. Educated Clayesmore School and Magdalene
College, Cambridge.
Research Professor of Geophysics, Durham University,
1988–91.
Professor of Geophysics, Durham University, 1966–88.
Murchison Medal of the Geological Society, 1977.

Let me first introduce myself. I was born in 1926, and my
younger brother Oliver and I were brought up in the small
Staffordshire village of Rough Close, just south of Stoke-
on-Trent. Our father worked on the commercial side of a
small pottery manufacturing company and Mother had
been a primary schoolteacher before marriage. Our schooling was at first local, but when I was twelve my brother and
I went away to Clayesmore School in Dorset. This was a
fairly free and easy school and our interest in outdoor
activities, such as walking and cycling in the beautiful
Dorset countryside, was encouraged. As a result of a small
school expedition to North Wales I was quite bitten by the
rock climbing bug although my attainments were modest.
My interest in science started much earlier, when I found
my mother's old school chemistry book, which was very
outdated no doubt, but fascinating to me. Later, at
Clayesmore, mathematics and physics displaced chemistry
as the focus of interest, after experience of some of the

pitfalls of practical chemistry. On leaving school there was National Service to be done, and I joined the Royal Signals. I was fortunate to be sent to East Africa, and was stationed for a year just under Kilimanjaro. With my mountaineering and exploring interests, this was an ideal posting and I enjoyed expeditions on Kilimanjaro, Mt Kenya and Mt Meru.

After demobilisation, I went up to Cambridge in 1948 to read mathematics, but after a few weeks changed to natural science with a view to physics. The mountaineering club was otherwise my main focus of interest as an undergraduate. The opportunity occurred to take part in a geological expedition to Spitzbergen in the summer of 1949 (and again in 1951). The result was that I ended up in the earth sciences rather than pure physics. My PhD topic concerned the use of geophysical methods to study the foundations of the Northern Pennines. I have never regretted my scientific migration to geophysics as it has enabled me to combine interests in physical science with outdoor activities. My work in earth science has also been in a most exciting period, with the plate tectonic revolution occurring during the 1960s, and the introduction of computers which are now central to most geophysical work.

I joined the Department of Geology in the University of Durham in 1954, first as a Research Fellow, then subsequently as Lecturer (1956), Reader, (1963) and Professor of Geophysics (1966). I retired as a full-time member of staff in 1988 but am continuing in a part-time research post. During my time in Durham I have been responsible with colleagues for the introduction of geophysics teaching, including an MSc course and a BSc course in geology and geophysics. I have maintained my early research interests in the deep structure of the British region, but have also been involved in marine geophysical investigations of the structure and evolution of the North Atlantic region, and in more theoretical studies of geodynamic processes such as the mechanism of plate tectonics and the origin of stress in the outer layers of the earth. At Durham, I have much enjoyed the combination of teaching and research, and in particular I have found it to be a great privilege and stimulus to work with research students.

My first introduction to Christianity was at home and during my early schooling. I remember being particularly enthralled when I first went to school by the short Scripture lessons outlining the Old Testament story from Abraham to Joshua. Later, my brother and I accompanied our parents to church in the nearby country village of Modershall, to which we used to walk on Sunday afternoons. As far as I am aware, I accepted the claims of Jesus to be the Son of God and the Truth of the Resurrection throughout my boyhood, but my interests in outdoor activities and science were much more central to me. I was confirmed at Clayesmore when I was about seventeen, and although the importance of the step we were taking was emphasised, I don't think it had much effect on me, and I certainly did not understand what it was all about. When I left school to join the forces, my lack of real commitment showed up as I rarely attended church during my National Service years, although I resumed on going up to Cambridge.

Another important strand came into play in my late teens and early twenties, during National Service and university. My mother had told us how King George V had read a chapter of the Bible each day of his life. In some inexplicable way, this encouraged me to start reading the Bible myself, particularly the New Testament. One point which particularly struck me was the way in which St Paul had written to the young churches as groups of believers whose lives had been radically changed and reorientated as a result of a living experience of Christ. This did not tally well with my own rather formal experience of Christianity. My concern was borne out when I got to know two committed Christian friends while training at Catterick Camp; one had been a Christian since childhood and the other had been converted during a confirmation service at Catterick. Later, at

Cambridge, the lives of friends from the Christian Union similarly testified to their real faith. It thus became apparent to me from reading the Bible and from the witness of Christians that there was something missing from my own commitment, but I did not realise what this was at that time.

I also had a significant experience during the Cambridge Spitzbergen expedition of 1949, when twelve of us spent most of the long vacation exploring the geology of part of this Arctic island. We were based on Billesfjord in the south-west of the island, but a party of five of us crossed the icecap, man-hauling two sledges, to explore the Stubendorf mountains and their geological structure. We were several days away from the base camp when this trip came to an abrupt end. All five of us were relaying one of the sledges up a steep snow slope on one of the Stubendorf glaciers, when the sledge broke through a snow bridge over a wide crevasse and pulled all of us down after it. The leader of the party broke his ankle in the fall (and later exhibited considerable courage in trekking back on skis over the icecap). The rest of us were unhurt as we landed on soft snow thirty to forty feet down the crevasse. We managed to climb out of the crevasse up a steep snow slope which had fallen in further along, but it took us most of a day to recover ourselves and our equipment. It was a very lucky escape, particularly since we had no radios and were quite out of touch with anyone else. That night, lying in our tents in the light Arctic summer night, I had a great experience of the goodness and providence of God, and I think this led me to a greater determination to seek him seriously. This time in Spitzbergen was also a turning-point in my career, as I had so much enjoyed the experience of combining science and exploration.

The greater turning-point, however, came during my second year as a research student, in autumn 1952. I had become increasingly concerned about my need for Christian commitment but did not understand how it could come about. The opportunity came with the week-long mission to the university organised by the Christian Union, with John Stott as the main speaker each evening. I attended the evening meetings in St Mary's Church and at the onset realized that here was the answer to my searching. During the talks I came to recognise how I had broken all the commandments in the deeper sense in which Jesus interpreted them, and that I had no power to do anything about it. As the message of the cross was explained, it was as if scales fell from my eyes. The cross had previously been an enigma to me, but now I understood for the first time how Jesus had died for me so that my sins could be forgiven and the barrier with God could thus be broken. At the end of one of the services, I yielded myself to Christ. As a result, joy and relief came flooding in. I have always looked back on this experience as my conversion, but I would not discount my previous experiences as they were all steps on the way.

Shortly afterwards I was faced by a testing time when I learned that difficulties in life do not all vanish on becoming a Christian, in fact to some extent they intensify. I was much helped by a small college Bible study group and by recruitment to help with a Christian summer camp for boys and with the Research Scientists' Christian Fellowship field courses for sixth-formers at Dale Fort in Pembrokeshire and elsewhere. It was at one of these courses that I met my wife Joyce, a botanist who was then working at the Freshwater Biological Station at Windermere. We were married in 1960 and now have three grown-up children. For most of our time at Durham we have belonged to St Nicholas Church, where I am now a Reader. The fellowship in this church has been very helpful and supportive, particularly during the last ten years when we have been experiencing renewal.

One of the potential stumbling-blocks for an earth scientist is the apparent conflict between the early Genesis account of creation and the scientific record of the development of the earth and life on it. Strangely, this problem has never caused me any serious difficulty or doubt, but nevertheless it looms large in the popular view of things. In simple terms, the problem arises as follows. The biblical record has sometimes been taken to imply a very short timespan of creation, perhaps about 6,000 years according to Archbishop Ussher who lived in the seventeenth century. In contrast, the geological timescale as determined by radiometric dating (using the decay of long-live radioactive isotopes such as uranium and thorium isotopes, potassium-40, rubidium-87 and carbon-14 for the youngest rocks) gives an age of about 4,400 million years for the formation of the earth and ages within this timescale for individual rocks. This timescale is consistent with the slow observed rate of geological processes. Even if one accepts an extended timescale, the early Genesis order of creation differs somewhat from the geologically inferred order, and the fossil record together with other biological evidence strongly supports an evolutionary origin of species rather than by separate events such as literal interpretation of the early chapters of Genesis might suggest.

Some Christians have attempted to resolve these difficulties by accepting the Genesis story as a literal scientific account of the origin and evolution of the earth and of life. Consequently, the scientific record is reinterpreted to fit in detail into the Genesis story. This requires great convolutions of the mind. An early example of someone who did this is Phillip Gosse (1810–88), a distinguished naturalist and also a leading member of the newly-founded Plymouth Brethren. He completely rejected the whole concept of Darwinian evolution and was forced to interpret the bands of fossils in the sedimentary rocks of England as if they had been created in the rocks in their present situation. This type of approach continues to the present day, and is called scientific creationism. It leads to the inference that the present-day physical and biological processes cannot generally be extrapolated back into the past, despite overwhelming evidence that in general they can. It thus makes an almost complete nonsense of the subject of historical geology, and implies that practically all earth scientists (as well as astronomers) have been barking up the wrong tree for the last 150 years or so.

Now scientific hypotheses and even theories are often wrong or imperfect, but good hypotheses are open to testing by observation or experiment. Science progresses in this way, and is dependent on new ideas, however strange. Scientists often have to admit that they are wrong, but when theories have been very heavily tested they form part of the body of scientific knowledge in which a good degree of confidence can be placed. An example of this is the methods of radiometric age dating. There are certainly some problems with the methods, which can, in consequence, sometimes give erroneous results, but these can often be recognised by inconsistency with results from other methods, and so on. But it is beyond plausibility to imply that the methods are systematically in error by a factor approaching 1 million, unless the observed rates of radioactive decay have so changed over the last 6,000 years. It is for reasons such as this that earth scientists, including many Christians among them, find it difficult to accept the scientific creationist approach, when there is a very much simpler and self-consistent explanation.

How can the viewpoints of the Christian and the earth scientist be reconciled? Personally, I have never had any serious difficulty over this apparent enigma, and did not find that it deterred me from seeking Christian truth, except possibly as an excuse. I regard the Genesis story, perhaps as far as chapter 11, as a sort of parable which reveals great basic truths about the purposes of God and the nature of mankind without any requirement for them to be taken strictly literally. It tells us that God created the universe and all life, how he created mankind in his own image (possibly via the evolutionary process), how mankind has the potential to explore and exploit the earth but has a basic ingrained tendency to do wrong, resulting in separation from God. The great basic truths which are revealed here are unattainable by scientific investigation. They are equally recognisable in the story whatever one takes the literary form to be. It is written in a form accessible to people of all ages, and should thus obviously not be taken as a scientific account of creation. The natural details of the history of creation, however, are available to ongoing scientific investigation of the sort which stems from the nature of creation and the God-given potential of mankind as revealed in Genesis and elsewhere in the Bible. On a more positive note, scientists are privileged to see how wonderfully the natural world is constructed, in all its complexity and beauty, and if they are Christians they respond by wonder and praise of the Creator.

The problems of science and faith discussed here have only arisen over the last hundred years or so, and consequently this has been a period of adjustment for our interpretation of some short but prominent parts of the Old Testament. Two practical issues which arise from these and related problems of science and faith need a mention. It seems important that Christians actively in contact with young people should be aware of the problems, and in particular should not press an interpretation of the early chapters of Genesis which conflicts with what is taught at school about the evolution of the earth and of life on it. Such a conflict may lead to a premature rejection of Christianity or to a compartmentalised understanding of Christian and scientific truth, which cannot be right. On the other hand, many older Christians who are not scientifically or otherwise academically inclined find it difficult and upsetting to adjust to a less literal interpretation. The last thing one would want to do would be to upset their faith, which is of much greater eternal significance than the propagation of scientific truth.

Scientists should be seeking the truth about the natural world in their work. Christians should also always seek the truth in all they do, including in their work. According to St John, Jesus was 'full of grace and truth', and he described himself to be 'the way, the truth and the life'. It is difficult, then, to see how there can be any real conflict between the creation by the Father, which can be explored by the scientist, and Christian truth as revealed in the Bible. Where there are apparent conflicts, then it seems that the reason must be our lack of understanding. And so, when confronted with other apparent conflicts over the Bible and natural knowledge of all kinds, the best approach seems to me to be 'reverent agnosticism', otherwise, we may raise unnecessary barriers which may deter others from seeking Jesus, who came to give those who come to him eternal life.

3

Credibility and Credo

Roy Peacock – Engineer

Professor Roy E. Peacock, PhD.
Educated Bristol Cathedral School, Cranfield Institute of Technology and St John's College, Cambridge.
Visiting Professor of Aerospace Science, University of Pisa.
Previously NAVAIR Professor in Aeronautics, Naval Postgraduate School, Monterey, California.
Director of Thermodyne Ltd, PoweResearch of Italy, The Carpenter's Trust
Chairman of Thermodyne Amos Ltd
Thirteenth Newton Memorial Lecturer.

Two questions arise whenever the words 'science' and 'faith' appear together: 'Hasn't science now disproved Christianity?' 'Aren't there such contradictions between the two that a person can't be both a scientist and a Christian?' Certainly, they would have been my questions when, as an emergent scientist, I could see nothing of relevance to my daily life in what I endured every Sunday in church-going. Prompted by little more than loyalty, my church life was a hangover from an earlier period as a professional choirboy. Church was a useful point of social contact, but little else. The more I saw of it, the greater was the magnetism of the world of science. It seemed to offer a rational alternative to the irrationality of one day in seven used in an activity insulated from all that was in the real world.

The final break came when I went to Cambridge as a research student, leaving the city and church of my childhood. I had already argued against the Christian claims made by open-air preachers on soap-boxes and the like, so the break was inevitable. If, at that time, I had known the popular version of the story of Galileo and his fight with the church, culminating with the verdict of his trial in June 1633—'vehemently suspected of heresy'—I would have said that as he, the reasonable scientist, was separated from the totalitarian regime of a reactionary group defending its vested interests, so I would take his position.

There followed four and a half years of research in the field of fluid mechanics, a time when the awe of being surrounded by great men resulted in trying to emulate their philosophy. I didn't question that they would be atheists. Indeed, my so-called agnosticism really was atheism—a life lived without reference to God at any point is a life that acts as if God does not exist and that is atheism in practice. Certainly, I had no idea that the men whose science I used day by day—Newton, Pascal, Leibnitz, and Boyle, for example, and Lord Kelvin, the father of thermodynamics, my own subject—were among a galaxy of scientists who had a conviction of God's existence that resulted in a dedication of their lives to him.

It was towards the end of my time at Cambridge that my next encounter with church came. A visit from a church-worker to tell my wife and me about a coming mission coincided with a promise I had made a retired clergyman to go to church, which I had begun doing once a month, merely to satisfy him.

The mission was all that I could have done without. I didn't like the speaker, the songs, or the company, so the situation had little promise. However, when the church-worker who had first visited our home made a gentle, but unavoidable, challenge to my wife that she could meet God, my earlier sense of indignation was replaced by the enquiry of the investigative scientist.

My wife's prayer ran along these lines: she admitted she was a sinner before God, she believed Jesus came to give her new life, he had died on the cross to make this possible and had risen from the dead to make it real to her. She asked that she might come to know God through this.

I was fascinated, realising that before me was the perfect scientific experiment to prove or disprove God's existence. Following an earlier conversation, I had all week been trying, through the normal processes of intellectualism, to establish God's existence or otherwise—the otherwise was preferred! Like so many before me, I had failed, but this experiment would bring a different and conclusive result.

My wife and I had been married for some years—I knew her. Her sincerity was beyond dispute. Now, I reasoned, if God exists he could not ignore such a prayer; he would come into her life and that would make an observable change. Hence, no change and I had my proof, no God— but if there was a change, then my atheism needed revision.

Her transformation, for such it was, brought me to the realisation that God was there, even if I'd never discovered him. That discovery took place at about 2.30 am the following morning. It was awesome for it transcended any analytical scientific appraisal I could make.

I saw a vision—I didn't believe in visions; I heard a voice—I certainly didn't believe in voices, and the words, 'The harvest is past, the summer is ended, and we are not saved' (Jer 8:20), thundered audibly about me. Soon I was converted, beginning a walk with Jesus Christ and discovering that the great divide between the Christian faith and scientific knowledge is a mirage promoted by a few noisy people. Truth is one; science, seeking for truth, can only ultimately draw the scientist to the reality of the Creator.

The scientist has two great opportunities. The first is to recognise that the remarkable cosmos, a portion of whose design he is exploring, or exploiting, has a remarkable Designer behind it. William Paley, an eighteenth-century theologian, related design, as he saw it in nature, to the inevitability of a Designer. The concept of an unbreakable design/Designer relationship is a powerful one, but it is not infallible. Aristotle saw design in the universe he knew and interpreted it in terms of all the heavenly bodies circulating the earth in circular orbits dictated by the crystalline spheres in which they were embedded. The supernatural element was added through the agency of an obliging team of angels who pushed the crystalline spheres around to produce the effect he observed.

For my part, perhaps because of my thermodynamics background, the place of entropy in the scheme of things is important. Our understanding of entropy goes back to the development of the steam engine and the attempts of Sadi Carnot to understand how to make it work better. He came to the staggering conclusion that for a steam engine to produce power, it not only transformed heat into work but, necessarily, threw some of the heat away. It was the rejected portion of the heat which became unavailable to the process of work generation that represented an increase of entropy—energy lost irretrievably to the atmosphere. Historically, that heat loss to the air around us has been radiated out into space. Because of the 'greenhouse' effect, more is being generated in the atmosphere than can escape, resulting in the predictions of global warming that make current news. Such global warming is a vivid illustration of the pattern of entropy growth. Much of the work of an engineer, particulary in the field of thermal power, is to reduce the heat loss from engines, while being aware that Carnot has shown it can never be eliminated.

From the concept of entropy and its application we get the clear understanding that the universe's energy bank is being redistributed in a manner which eventually destroys its usefulness. The picture speaks of an end and a beginning for the universe.

There has been much argument about the permanence of the universe we inhabit: Aristotle thought that it was ever-lasting and, more recently, Stephen Hawking has published a book which has caught the public imagination, in which he suggests an unending cosmos. This point is emphasised by Carl Sagan, who uses it to question the existence of a Creator in a foreword to Hawking's book. But the impermanence of the universe is written into astronomical observations from antiquity. Supernova—stars in their death throes—are bodies emitting massive amounts of light. Possibly the earliest recorded, which was also chronicled by Chinese astronomers, is in the Bayeux Tapestry. But the first entirely reliable observation was by Tycho Brahe, the man whose experimental measurements were essential for Kepler to conclude that planetary motion was elliptical, not circular as the Greeks had thought. A supernova is, then, a clear indication that somewhere, something is coming to an end.

A further sign of a universe wearing out—entropy taking its toll—is in black holes, singularities in the universe that are cul-de-sacs in time and space. If they exist, it is generally thought that they are the final result in a process of decay of massive star formations—dead ends, it might be said!

Now, observations like these tell us that there is an inevitable progress in time from order to disorder; that is, an increase in entropy, a movement from a beginning to an end. In fact, this becomes a definition of time—the concept of entropy increase is, in basic scientific terms, possibly the only statement we have of what time is and which way it progresses. Anything that is eternal does not have time as a component. So the fact that we have a commodity called time, which only goes in one direction, is a further sign that we are going through a time-measurable process which has limits.

Of a beginning, there is also evidence. The echo of a Big Bang, predicted years before it was measured, was discovered accidentally: galactic red-shift, a change in the colour of galaxies of stars as we see them, akin to the change in sound of a siren on an emergency vehicle as it passes a person, is evidence of an initial event, a creation.

There has been much heated argument about a creation and an end to all things and these are central in Christian thinking. From my early Christian days, I never doubted these postulates, but it is an encouragement to see them confirmed by scientific observation. I don't necessarily think that the end of which the Bible speaks will be coincident with a maximisation of entropy—that would be a pretty miserable situation, not the moment of glory that Christians are promised—but I am glad to know the scientific confirmation that things cannot go on for ever. Applied in my personal life, it is a remarkable spur to do something about it.

It could be concluded that the inevitable increase of entropy has nothing to do with God: we are observing inanimate nature doing the thing that nature does. Yet within this chaotic breakdown of order we find that there can still be order—wakes shed from ships or aircraft producing beautiful spirals of pattern, intricate vortices, and fractal images with their repetitive patterns, provide examples. To me, this is a strong indication of the governing hand of a thinking God. Chaos theory represents a new scientific discipline. It indicates a growth of disorder from order, big perturbations arising out of small perturbations. The so-called 'butterfly effect', in which the minute disturbances of a butterfly's wings could initiate a major weather storm on the other side of the world, is based upon the idea that the small atmospheric disturbances of the wing result in progressively larger disturbances. While any one element in the chain of events follows well known, deterministic laws, the entire process goes beyond anything that can be predicted by these laws. The deterministic laws, as we know them, don't tell the whole story. Applied, for example, to the cyclic motion of our solar system we are entirely without any explanation of why its clockwork pattern is maintained when it is known to have perturbations.

Somehow, the solar system is being held together when it should be flying apart. At that point I am bound to say that God is holding it, but since he must be purposeful if he is God, then he is doing so for a purpose.

And that brings me to the purpose and to the scientists's second great opportunity. It is to discover that the Designer, God, is an interventionist: he takes a direct active interest both in the scientists's exploration of his science and in the scientist himself. His interventionist nature is seen not just in the esoteric things like entropy, chaos and perturbations but, more important, in the way lives are lived. It is revolutionary to discover that his active interest is not restricted to those professions we like to identify as 'Christian'—in the church or the field of medicine, for example. It transforms the working life to know that God is interested, can be involved and may be glorified through it.

I had been a Christian for some years before it occurred to me that the Lord was interested in my working life. Being in the academic world, I found it useful to pray before giving a lecture—although I was probably motivated by pure terror! But then I became convinced that God was interested in my scientific research, at that time an investigation into unsteady air-flow effects. The work employed one student, one small test facility and £1,000. It didn't seem worthwhile to bother God with it.

My dedication was to commit the research to the Lord on a daily basis and to discipline myself with the conditioned reflex that, whenever a crisis arose—a regular occurrence—I would pray specifically about the issue. Now, this was not meant to be a lazy man's way of doing a day's work; motivation was not reduced, neither was my responsibility which, eventually, was for a large team and programme, in academic terms. In fact, since I recognised that my scientific work was part of my life of Christian expression, I saw a greater need for my dedication to doing the best job possible: as Galileo put it, to be 'lifted up to the ultimate goal of our efforts, that is to the love of the divine artificer'.

Following my dedication, things began to happen in my laboratory which certainly were not in my previous experience—I saw the application of faith affecting my scientific life. One example will suffice.

My programme of experimental research included taking measurements of rapidly changing flow fields within some rotating machinery. With the advance of electronics and micro-miniaturisation used in today's instruments, such measurements can be made without difficulty. At that time, so far as we knew, no one had successfully mastered the technique, so we had to design and develop our own instrumentation.

All electronic and electrical systems generate unwanted signals—a television or radio never reproduces precisely the transmitted programme, but adds what is called 'noise'. It is the same in the electronics used in scientific experiments and, for the instrument to be useful, the signal it handles must be very much stronger than the noise it generates. We worked happily with a signal that was up to 100 times stronger than the unwanted noise, until one day, the noise swamped the signal.

Because of the seriousness of the problem, all other work was stopped until the difficulty was resolved. Every available team member was engaged in finding a solution. After two and a half days, we still had no solution and the timetable of our programme was being endangered. At this point, I recalled my commitment to pray about problems, retired to my office and did so. Returning to the laboratory, I heard one of the mechanics, a man we didn't take much notice of, saying that he had an idea, but to test it would require something he would have with him after lunch.

Following the lunch break, I saw him cycling back from his home with a small package in his hand. It turned out to be a portable radio which he proceeded to tune to various stations until he found a musical programme. We watched, bemused, as we saw the trace on the cathode ray oscilloscope, which recorded the noise, faithfully following in form and amplitude the music from the radio. It was immediately evident that our system had an unscreened piece of electrical lead which happened to act as a tuned aerial to one of the British Broadcasting Corporation stations, a problem that was successfully addressed in moments.

Analysing this incident, the cynic may say that I am reporting a coincidence and such a childish mistake—for it was—would have been located sooner or later in any case. We would certainly have had to resolve the problem eventually or stop our experimental programme, but the fact remains that our discovery took place immediately following prayer. The scientist does not deal in coincidences: his is the world of mathematical analysis and, in assessing the likelihood of events taking place, of statistics and probability. He would enquire what was the probability of discovering the error immediately following the prayer and, if prayer was not a contributory feature, he might conclude that there was just as much chance of reaching the correct diagnosis at any other time in the two and a half days. In other words, the statistical probability of this event occurring as it did, immediately following prayer, was very small. In taking his enquiry further, the scientist would want to examine a range of such 'coincidences'. When they are all stacked up, the improbability of such events, linked to prayer, is enormous—unless there is a God behind them, answering the prayer.

Every profession has its career structure and most people are interested in moving up their personal ladder of achievement. Few refuse the opportunity of promotion.

During a particularly productive phase of work, I was advised unofficially that my name was being forwarded for a position with a measure of recognition and prestige. I didn't decline! The process took about a year to go through the system. References, board meetings and various discussions were part of the procedure. Although I was not supposed to know that my name had been put forward, I was kept informed of events as they took place. The news was good—I was a happy man. One and a half days before the last board meeting to ratify the decision before it was announced to me and the world, I was praying when, clearly, I knew that the appointment would be denied me. Within two days, the selection board also knew as it made the decision.

In due course, there was an unexpected development— the offer of a similar appointment with another organisation. Since the nature of the job would involve a number of changes I wasn't anxious to make, I declined. A couple of months later, while my wife and I were staying with friends, my host's wife shared a word she felt she needed to tell me: 'Behold, I have opened a door before you which no man shall close—and you will pass through it' (Rev 3:8). Over the next nine months, the same word was repeated to me once a month by a series of people, none of whom knew of the existence of any previous reference of this type. Eventually, convinced that God was directing me towards the offer I had already refused, I made a tentative approach to the originators of the invitation. My discovery was that they had kept the appointment open!

The Christian life isn't all about being successful; rather, it is about being formed by God for his purposes. For this, obedience is vital, but it is obedience to his word, not our inclination.

To facilitate negotiations between the US and British governments on exchange of scientific information, I was invited to join a small team including senior members of the Scientific Civil Service and a senior industrial observer. The four-man team spent some time at a military research establishment in Kentucky and the negotiations took place in a series of buildings separated from each other by such large distances that we were issued with a car and military driver. The schedule of meetings was very tight.

While being driven from one location to the next during

the talks, we encountered a rain storm of prodigious proportions. The road quickly flooded and the car was soon driving in deep water. Spray entered the engine compartment, flooding the electrical components so that the engine stopped. In such circumstances, there is no use in opening the bonnet, since that only lets in more rain and, from experience, I knew that we could do no more than hope the heat of the engine would eventually dry out the electrical components. Several attempts to restart the engine failed but I had not accounted for the driver who, although silent up to this point, was clearly a resourceful person. Gripping the steering wheel and addressing the general area of the dashboard, he commanded in a loud voice, 'In the name of Jesus Christ, I command you to go.'

Now, the car was full of scientists who knew that the engine was wet and that it could not go—the scientific proof lay in the fact of several failed attempts. When the engine then fired immediately and we continued to our destination, the car was full of rather silent scientists trying to work it out!

Perhaps the scientist is at an advantage in the matters of the Christian life: he cannot dismiss things as coincidence or ignore what is going on around him, while maintaining his scientific credibility. He is, of course, aware that the fact there appears to be an answer to prayer on one occasion does not, of itself, prove anything. But when prayer is seen to be efficient in life, he can have confidence in it. In a way, it is rather like our understanding of the basic laws of science. They aren't laws in the sense that they declare what is going to happen, prescriptive—as legislation on the statute books of nations—rather, they are descriptive, summing up the body of observation made by scientists. But the value of these laws lies not in that they comprise a succinct piece of history but that we reckon to rely upon them—and so we use them in a predictive sense. The whole of science, technology and industry is geared to this.

Using the example of entropy once more, no one can say

that it never could reduce—the relevant law has only said that a reduction within a system has never been observed—but, if it should be seen to reduce, then we would have to abandon science as we know it. Meanwhile, the scientist lives by faith in the fact of the law's accuracy.

Similarly, the Christian can have confidence that as God has answered prayer before, he will continue so to do—that is his nature and we can have faith in it. But the Christian, scientist or not, doesn't make that statement on the grounds of statistical probability; he does so on the basis that he has the privilege of an ongoing relationship with an interventionist God who intervened in life for him through the cross.

Rather than disprove Christianity, science offers the methods of observation and analysis that support the claims of the Christian life. That is why it is entirely conceivable for a scientist to be a Christian without losing any of his scientific or Christian credibility. In spite of the popular opinion of Galileo, pictured as the role model of scientists of the world standing in opposition to the Christian church, Galileo was a man who prayed, sought to know the mind of God and encouraged others similarly. It is when scientific endeavour and the Christian faith came together in Johannes Kepler that, upon discovering the ellipticality of planetary orbits to confirm Copernicus' view of a heliocentric solar system, he exclaimed, 'O God, I am thinking thy thoughts after thee.'

4

A God Big Enough

John Houghton – Meteorologist

Sir John T. Houghton, CBE, MA, DPhil, F Inst Phys, FRS.
Born 1931. Educated Rhyl Grammar School and Jesus College, Oxford.
Director, Appleton Laboratory, 1979–83; Professor of Atmospheric Physics, Oxford University, 1976–83; Director-General of the Meteorological Office since 1983.
Honorary Fellow, Jesus College, Oxford, since 1983.
President, Royal Meteorological Society, 1976–78.
Vice-President, World Meteorological Organization since 1987.
Chairman, Scientific Assessment of Intergovernmental Panel on Climate Change, 1988/90.
Chairman, Royal Commission on Environmental Pollution since 1992.

When people discover that I am involved with weather forecasting and also that I am a Christian, I am often asked if I believe that there is any point in praying about the weather—praying for rain, for instance, when it is badly needed. I reply that I believe it is entirely sensible and meaningful to pray about the weather as, indeed, it is to pray about other things. But I also say that my belief in the meaningfulness of prayer in no way alters my determination as a scientist to develop the very best means of weather forecasting, nor does it cause me to doubt that the behaviour of weather systems follows deterministic scientific laws.

One of the outstanding successes of science over the last thirty years has been that of weather prediction through the use of computer models of the atmospheric circulation. Let me explain how these models are employed in what is called numerical weather prediction. First of all, observations of the state of the atmosphere over the globe are received from orbiting satellites, from balloons, from ships, from automatic recording stations and from conventional land stations. These are brought together every twelve hours to make the best description possible of the atmosphere's state at that time. Starting from that initial state, the computer solves the appropriate equations of motion and produces a forecast for the whole globe for ten or more days ahead; for this task the largest and fastest computer available is required.

Meteorologists have no doubt that the atmosphere is basically a deterministic system, in other words, that the atmosphere's future behaviour is determined by its present state and by the laws of physics. This does not mean that weather prediction can ever become an exact science. One of the main reasons for this is that the atmosphere is what is known as a chaotic system—a technical term for a system in which developments occur which are extremely sensitive to the initial conditions.

For the atmosphere, the implications of 'chaos' are such that, as Edward Lorenz, one of the world's leading meteorologists, has explained,[1] the flapping of a butterfly's wings somewhere in the atmosphere can have a noticeable effect on weather developments thousands of miles away. No conceivable observing system could record the atmosphere in that sort of detail. Not only are there practical limits to our ability to measure and observe, there are also fundamental limits. Meteorologists have a great deal to learn about the science of 'chaos' and its implications for predictability. Our current expectation is that we have a good chance of predicting the general pattern of climate change which might occur over the next hundred years or so due to man's activities, for instance, through the burning of fossil fuels, but that our ability to forecast detailed weather cannot extend to more than perhaps two weeks.

My belief, on the one hand, in the reality of prayer and, on the other, in the scientific study of the material world as a deterministic system may seem at first to be contradictory. At best, it may seem that my life as a scientist and my religious life are in separate compartments. This, however, is not the case. It is very important to me that the two strands of my life, as a scientist and as a Christian, are brought together side by side and, so far as it is possible, intertwined. How, therefore, can the idea, on the one hand, that God is active in the world and, on the other, that events are governed by scientific laws be reconciled? The clue, I believe, is in making God big enough. To do that it is necessary to really stretch our ideas and imagination. I believe science can help in this.

Think, for instance, about the universe and its utterly fantastic size and complexity. Planet earth is one of the smaller planets orbiting around a modest-sized star we call the sun. The sun is just one of 100 billion (10^{11}) stars in the galaxy to which it belongs; some of the brightest of these stars we see in the Milky Way. Within the whole universe there are upwards of a billion (10^9) galaxies. To travel to our sun 150 million kilometres away would take just 8 minutes if travelling at the speed of light. To reach the edge of the galaxy would take 100,000 years, and to reach the edge of the universe, if that were possible, about 10 billion (10^{10}) years. These are completely mind-boggling numbers.

As astronomers have probed the universe with their telescopes—optical and radio telescopes on the ground, X-ray, ultra-violet and infra-red telescopes out in space—they have been able to discover a great deal about the processes going on in the stars, the galaxies and the space in between. Many new objects have been identified; quasars, pulsars and black holes. One of the remarkable features of this story of discovery is that the physical laws which govern what is going on in widely different parts of the universe are the same physical laws which describe events here on earth. In fact, a major achievement of modern science has been the way in which it has been possible to apply the physics of the very smallest components of matter (which are as many orders of magnitude smaller than us as the universe is larger) to reach some understanding of what is known as the Big Bang—that singular event over ten billion years ago from which the expansion of the universe began.

A similar and perhaps even more remarkable story can be told about the structure of life, with the many complex and interdependent molecules that make up even the simplest living cell. Although there remains a tremendous amount to learn about many parts of these scientific stories, all of us, scientists and laymen alike, cannot fail to be impressed with the vastness, the complexity, the intricacy and the order of it all.

We all know what it means to create something—a painting, a three course meal, a computer programme—we are creating all the time. Just try to imagine the skill and power of the One who has conceived and created the universe and who continues to maintain it in being. He is the God we are trying to think about. The size, the complexity, the beauty and the order we find in the universe are expressions of the greatness, the beauty and the orderliness of the Creator.

How does all this tie up with the scientific description of the world and the laws which we deduce from that description? The conflict which is often thought to be present between the scientific description and the description of God as Creator arises, I believe, from a misunderstanding of what both descriptions are about. Rather than a conflict there is a close connection; the order and consistency we find in our science can be seen as reflecting orderliness and consistency in the character of God himself.

Created along with the universe is its framework of space and time. This means that when we think of the Creator we think of him as being outside the space and time dimensions of our world and of our experience. That does not mean, as some suggest, that God is not present and active in the world; but it does mean that he is not confined by it. Because God's activity continually pervades the world, I do not like to talk about God intervening in our world. Although he may seem to be in some events more than others, he is in a real sense present with us all the time.

In the Gospels we find Jesus emphasising God's control over the world and God's concern for even the smallest events. A sparrow cannot fall to the ground without our heavenly Father's knowledge (Mt 10:29). Jesus encouraged his followers to look at events and circumstances in terms of God's activity. He chided the Pharisees, the religious leaders of the day, for their blindness. When they wanted to forecast the weather, their interpretation of the sky was quite good, he told them, but their interpretation of the events of the times was seriously lacking (Mt 16:3). In other words, their meteorological science was effective, but they were blind towards any appreciation of God's activity in the world.

As a Christian believer, therefore, I am looking for more than scientific order and consistency in the world and the events that surround me. Because I believe that God is also a Person who is concerned about the people he has created and is therefore concerned even about me and my small world, I am looking for evidence of God's activity in these events and circumstances. I am also looking for answers to my prayers. As I have argued in more detail elsewhere,[2] I believe that God is big enough to provide this double order and consistency. On the one hand, we can look for order and consistency in the scientific description of events, and on the other hand, for order and consistency in a description of those events in terms of God's activity.

It is on the subject of answers to prayer that the sceptic

can be at his most critical. Christians seem to argue that God always answers their prayers even if such argument flies in the face of the facts. They pray for healing for instance. If recovery occurs that is a positive answer. If it does not, God still answers; he knows, they say what is best. How in the face of such blind faith, the sceptic will exclaim, is it possible to establish objective facts in a scientific manner? Is not the Christian indulging in a heavy dose of wishful thinking?

To question in this manner, however, is to misunderstand the nature of prayer. Prayer is not going to God with a shopping list. It is not looking for magic, rubbing the lamp and making wishes. God is not a great impersonal potentate, nor a grand Santa Claus, but he is a Person with whom we human beings can form a relationship. The exercise of prayer is the means whereby that relationship is developed. A model which Christians find helpful for that relationship is that of us as God's children communicating with him as our Father. A child is constantly asking for things. Because the child does not understand enough of his needs to know what is good for him, his father will grant some of his requests and not grant others. We can expect and want God to treat our prayers in a similar way.

Prayer is not something I find easy; I sometimes envy those much more pious in disposition than I to whom it seems to be second nature. But it is an activity which, like many things we do, becomes more real and meaningful with practice. The practice of prayer has various forms. Let me divide them into the formal and the informal. Formal prayer is presented by groups of Christians meeting together for worship in church or elsewhere. I also engage in more or less formal prayer when my wife and I each day have a short prayer time when we commit to God particular problems or the needs of particular people. I also attempt to practise more or less formal prayer on my own, although that is a discipline I cannot say I have mastered. Informal prayer I define as the bringing to God, often very briefly and without it being in any way obvious to others who may be around, a particular need, a problem of the moment or a special expression of gratitude or thanks. That sort of prayer is very important to me, not only because I find it a source of strength in the stress and tumble of everyday living, but also because it is an important way in which my faith is integrated with and woven into the rest of my life. It is probably the sort of prayer to which the apostle Paul was referring when he urged the readers of the Epistle to the Thessalonians to pray without ceasing (1 Thess 5:17).

Those who are engaged in full-time Christian work often speak of answers to prayer which have come through unusual events. Over a number of years I was closely involved with the setting up of a residential centre in Oxford for students from overseas. To those of us involved it seemed a very Christian enterprise for which it was entirely appropriate to ask for God's help. And help came. Money came in from unexpected sources just when it was needed. A surprising turn of events enabled us to buy a very suitable property for which we had been negotiating but which we thought had been lost to us. The coupling of our prayers with these circumstances encouraged us to believe that we were partners with God in what we were trying to do; not that we should look for God only in the unusual events which may occur from time to time and which may provide a particular stimulus to faith. God is also there in the usual—I feel that it is important to attempt to look at all the circumstances that surround me from the standpoint of my relationship with God. There have, for instance, been occasions when I have prayed about parti- cular problems or events in my scientific work. And I believe these prayers have been answered. Although in the very nature of things these answers are of a personal kind and not easy to describe to others in an objective way, they are nevertheless real.

God's work in the world is more often than not through people; that is certainly true of God's work in my own life.

This means that as people we have a great responsibility—we need to be sensitive to what God wants from us. For those of us who are scientists it means that we need to face up to the question of what is the value of our scientific work and to try, as far as we are able, to ensure that the science for which we have some responsibility is properly used.

Very early in the Bible (Gen 1:28) we are told that man has been made in the image of God and that he has been placed on the earth to be its steward. We should not, therefore, be afraid to grasp the resources and capabilities we have been given, using them, first, to express worship for the Creator, and second, to care for the world and the human beings within it in ways which are consistent with the declared wishes and purpose of the One for whom we are acting as steward. A big challenge currently faced by scientists—especially by those of us who are involved with the science of the environment—is the concern about the climate change which will occur next century largely because of our increased burning of fossil fuels. We first need to understand what change in climate may take place. But our responsibility as scientists does not stop there; we also need to be thoroughly involved in the debate regarding what action can be taken to limit the amount of change, to alleviate the problems arising from change and to assist those who will have to cope with substantial change.

When thinking of God's work in the world, a particularly perplexing problem is the problem of suffering. I do not think I am unusual in finding it a real difficulty. My first wife, Margaret, fought cancer for ten years; eventually she died from it at the age of fifty-four. We prayed a lot for healing, as did many of our friends. Were those prayers answered or not? I believe they were, in two ways.

First, there were the times of particular crisis when the right medical treatment was needed and needed urgently. On many of these occasions, from the various possibilities available it was not obvious what should be done for the best. Advice came at different times from different people and different quarters, but each time we felt content that the medical course being taken was right and indeed the best available. After all, the practice of medicine is a direct use of the material resources which God has provided for us in his creation. Healing through medical means is just as much God's work as healing by any other means, natural or supernatural. The combination of medicine and prayer is therefore entirely appropriate when tackling disease.

The second way in which we felt our prayers were answered was that God provided strength to face the battle—physical, mental and spiritual—involved in coping with the cancer. This was particularly the case towards the end when we had to face the fact that the cancer was winning. The quality of Margaret's faith and trust in God was truly remarkable and an inspiration to all who met her during that period. We were very conscious of the power of God through prayer to transform our circumstances and suffering into some lasting good.

After Margaret died I questioned my belief in resurrection and the afterlife. Looking at her cold lifeless body, it seemed impossible that she could live on; but then it also seemed impossible that her strong faith and radiant spirit could just fade away into nothingness. I realised the key to my belief was the resurrection of Jesus. The historical evidence alone is not the basis of that belief. As a scientist, however strong that evidence seems to be, it cannot on its own compensate for the scepticism I am bound to feel about dead bodies coming to life. But there is other evidence too. There is the testimony of millions of Christians over the centuries, from the first disciples who carefully recorded their experiences in the books of the New Testament, to that of Margaret, still very vivid in my memory. And there is the personal experience I have of Jesus as one who is alive in my experience today. The Jesus I meet in the pages of the Gospels is the One I meet as I attempt to communicate with God in prayer and the One I meet through the lives and conversations of others in the Christian community.

When thinking about resurrection, an analogy I find helpful is one based on the computer.[3] Computer hardware consists of the silicon chips, the wires, the disc stores, the keyboards and tape decks with which the input can be introduced, and the screens and printers which display the output. The software consists of the programmes which manipulate (and in sophisticated computers learn from) the input data and provide the means to organise the output and the contents of the store. The software is no use by itself; it needs hardware on which to act and through which to be expressed. The hardware has a limited life; in time it wears out. The software is not so perishable—it can be transferred to new hardware although it will still bear characteristics of the hardware for which it was originally written. New, more advanced hardware can provide more scope for the software, enabling not only larger calculations to be carried out but perhaps providing new capabilities. Our bodies are like the hardware providing input devices (our senses) and output devices (our limbs, speech etc), and processor and storage (our brains). Some of the software is built in from the start; it is genetically determined. Other software is continuously generated throughout our lives from interaction with our environment and with other people, from our thought processes and our choices and from interaction with the hardware. Our body, in due course, wears out like any other hardware. In resurrection, the Christian hope is for a new body which will have sufficient continuity with the old to take on the old software and which will give us new means of expression.

This computer analogy illustrates a way in which scientific thinking and thinking about faith can be brought together. I have tried to pursue elsewhere other, not dissimilar, analogies.[4] An important characteristic of faith is that it brings together and gives meaning to seemingly very different parts of life and experience. There are two ways in which we can learn about and relate to God. He has revealed himself in the world around us with all its order, intricacy and fascination. He has also revealed himself in the Person of Jesus. Think for a moment about the appreciation of depth which is contained in a scene viewed with both eyes rather than with one eye, or the depth which stands out in pairs of pictures viewed through a stereoscope. Objects appear solid; estimates of distance can be made. Putting the two revelations of God together is like having binocular vision. A new depth and reality are created in our appreciation of the world around us and of God himself. We also appreciate how much more there is to explore, both in the world and in God.

Notes

[1] J. Gleick, *Chaos* (Heinemann: London, 1987).
[2] J.T. Houghton, *Does God Play Dice?* (Inter-Varsity Press: Leicester, 1988).
[3] *Ibid*, p 127.
[4] *Ibid*.

5

A Talent for Science

Ghillean Prance – Botanist

Professor Ghillean T. Prance, MA, D Phil, Fil Dr, F Inst Biol.
Born 1937. Educated Malvern College and Keble College, Oxford.
New York Botanical Garden (1963–88), becoming Senior Vice-President for Science and Director of the Institute of Economic Botany.
Director, Royal Botanic Gardens, Kew, since 1988.
Visiting Professor, Reading University; Visiting Professor, Yale University, 1983–88.
Foreign Member of the Academies of Science of Brazil, Denmark and Sweden.
President, Association of Tropical Biology, 1979–80.
President, American Association of Plant Taxonomists, 1984–85.
President, Systematics Association, 1989–91.
Distinguished Service Award, New York Botanical Garden, 1986.
Diploma Honra ao Merito, Instituto Nacional de Pesquisas da Amazonia, 1978.
Linnean Medal, 1990.

The problems of my interest in both botany and the Christian faith began at an early age—I was six years old and we were living in the Isle of Skye. One Sunday morning as I was walking to church with my parents I spotted a roadside flower that interested me and picked it. It was a harebell or blue bell of Scotland (*Campanula rotundifolia*). I was then in trouble for disgracing the family in public by doing such a thing on the Sabbath. After church I was sent to my room without lunch. My annoyance was not so much that I was punished, but that my parents were being unfair, since they did not really adhere to the strict local customs; their justification was that the opinion of the neighbours and of our hostess, cousin Margaret, was what mattered. I am glad to say that in the long run that misadventure did not deter my interest either in botany or the church.

I was brought up in a nominally Christian environment where church was an important part of family life, and many of our activities revolved around the parish life of a small Cotswold village church. However, it was not until my first term at Oxford University that I made a firm commitment to the Christian faith and the teaching of the Bible. This was through the ministry of the Oxford University Christian Union (OICCU). After hearing the gospel preached on my first two Sundays at Oxford, I accepted Christ on the third, and I soon became an active member of OICCU and served on their executive committee as prayer secretary.

The good teaching received there and from Saint Ebb's Church in Oxford gave me a firm grounding for the future. After leaving Oxford I spent twenty-five years in the USA and Brazil, during which time I was a member of the First Baptist Church, White Plains, New York. In Brazil, in the course of my botanical fieldwork, I had the opportunity to travel widely on the mission field and to support the activity of local churches, especially the First Baptist Church of Manaus. As tropical deforestation has accelerated I have become progressively more active in ecological issues, and as a consequence also in creation theology and the Christian basis for environmental protection. I am currently a member of Holy Trinity Church, Hounslow, where I am happy to work with a church that has been renewed by the Holy Spirit.

The first problem that I faced on my conversion was which path my future should take. I was naturally anxious to serve my newly found Lord to the best of my ability, and soon after my conversion I began to consider whether I was being called to a full-time ministry. In fact, I went as far as a Church of England selection committee where I was accepted as a candidate for ordination.

It was the wisdom and council of my future father-in-law, himself an Anglican clergyman, that was most helpful at this stage of my career. He pointed out the talents I had in botany and that from as early as I could remember I had collected plants. At school I had few botany lessons because my biology master said that I already knew more than I was likely to learn in his classes! Actually, I learned a great deal on field trips with him all over the British Isles, and this gave me the strong botanical grounding that has helped me throughout the rest of my career. My father-in-law explained that this knowledge of botany was a talent given from God and that I should use it to the glory of the Lord. He expounded to me in a helpful way Romans 12: 4–7, about the use of spiritual gifts, and it was perhaps at that time that I began to recognise my botanical background as a God-given gift. The result was that I made a positive decision to serve God through a career in botany and to seek to do it well as part of my Christian testimony.

I have never regretted that decision; it has been confirmed in the many ways in which I have had opportunities to serve the Lord during the course of my work as an Amazonian explorer botanist. There is no doubt that I have been a better, more dedicated, and successful botanist as a result of my Christian faith; my faith and desire to serve the Lord through the quality of my work has helped me to work harder and more conscientiously. An attitude that has

always troubled me is that of Christians who are too busy
with church activities and other Christian pursuits to perform
their jobs satisfactorily. That cannot be a good testimony to
a living faith in Jesus Christ, yet it is a frequent occurence. I
was strongly advised by my father-in-law to strive for
excellence in my studies and my career; I have always been
extremely grateful for his wise, yet at the time difficult,
advice to follow.

Perhaps the reconciliation between faith and science is
easier for a biologist than for those in other areas of
science, for biologists have the opportunity to study the
working of creation. The question that is always asked of a
biologist with a Christian faith is, 'How do you reconcile
your belief in God with the theory of evolution?' For me,
that has never been a real difficulty.

I was brought up in evolutionary thought from an early
age and before I was fifteen years old had studied in the
field the camouflage of moths on tree bark, the pollination
of bird's foot trefoil, and many other examples of evolution. I first read Darwin's *Origin of Species* just before
going to Malvern College as a thirteen-year-old. The
wonders of creation are just as great whether God created
in a single step or used the gradual mechanism of evolution. My subsequent research on intricately coevolved
relationships between plants and animals of the Amazon
rainforest has confirmed rather than reduced my awe at
the greatness of creation. The *Epiphyllum* cactus flower
which I studied has a tubular flower which is eight inches
long, with nectar at the base of the tube. Its hawkmoth
pollinator has a tongue eight inches in length with which
it can reach the nectar at the bottom of the tubular
flower, providing a perfect match between the morphology
of the plant and the insect because they have coevolved
together. To me this is both a fine example of coevolution
and of the perfection of God's creation. God saw that it
was good!

The scientist Christian can get into some amusing and

difficult situations. During my travels around Amazonian Brazil I have always looked for local churches and sought to link up with them and encourage their work in any way possible. However, there is not always a clear understanding that a scientist can also be a Christian. Any foreigner entering a local church is automatically assumed to be a missionary. On my first Sunday in the First Baptist Church of Manaus, Brazil, I was asked by a deacon for biographical details in order to be welcomed during the service by the pastor. I explained to my questioner that I was a botanist from the New York Botanical Garden working with the local research institute and that I was also a Christian layman. After writing extensive notes he asked, 'What mission did you say you were from?' Again, I thought that I explained my situation well, and he left with his notes. I was asked by the pastor to stand and was introduced to the congregation as Dr Prance from the 'New York Botanical Missionary Society'! It is sad that even in a large city church a foreign Christian is automatically associated with full-time mission work. Where are all the Christian laymen? Do they go on holiday from church when they travel as tourists or on business to Manaus or other tropical cities? I have been blessed so often on my travels through attending worship in a foreign city where I did not understand a word of the language. The unity in Christ is the same.

I once spent a few weeks in the northern frontier town of Brazil, Boa Vista (the capital of Roraima State). I attended the local Baptist church which had a wonderful pastor who befriended me. On my last Sunday there, he asked me to preach at the evening service, and I gladly accepted. He stood up in the pulpit and introduced me with the usual nice words, and then informed his congregation that here was the proof that man was not descended from monkeys. A biological scientist was about to preach. As I got up to follow this introduction I was thinking of 1 Corinthians 8:13: 'Therefore, if food is a cause of my brother's falling, I will never eat meat, lest I cause my brother to fall.' I was careful to affirm that church where I could, and to preach the gospel faithfully without touching on any controversial subject that might have caused my brothers in the church to stumble, and as a result there was considerable response to my preaching.

Perhaps one of the most difficult classes I have ever taught was in response to the request of a pastor of a fast growing, theologically conservative church in Manaus. It had reached the stage in its development where, for the first time, teenage members were entering university. The pastor expressed his concern to me and to a Brazilian scientist member of the church (Warwick Kerr, a well known geneticist) that many of the young church members dropped out of church when they went to university because of the conflict between their conservative theology and the evolutionary and atheist beliefs of their university teachers. We were asked by this wise pastor to teach a Sunday school course on creation and evolution, amid considerable criticism from his church members. In the course we looked at both the scientific details and the biblical teachings on creation: it helped this group of young people to use their intellectual abilities for matters of faith and prepared them for the university scene. Here we were helping to harmonise science and Christian faith for a group of people who had come from the opposite end of the spectrum to me, through a strong faith in the Creator rather than an extensive knowledge and interest in his creation. Our experiment worked because when I return to that church today, I always meet some of that class who have survived their launch into the world without becoming part of it. At times it was not easy for us to take barbed words from some of the church deacons, but we helped to produce a new generation of thinking Christians in that church, and they continue the work with today's youth.

Conservation and stewardship

I first went to the Amazon region in 1963 to study plants and to collect material for basic taxonomic work. During the first ten years of my exploration in Amazonia I was privileged to travel widely and had a wonderful opportunity to carry out research in the region, with little concern for environmental issues. It was a time of learning about the plants and the animals with which they interact. The more I understood complicated pollination mechanisms by bats, beetles, birds and butterflies, and the ways in which plants defend themselves against the hoards of leaf-eating predators, the more I marvelled at creation. By 1973, however, the situation in Amazonia had changed drastically and large-scale development, accompanied by massive destruction of the forest, had begun. For example, the TransAmazon Highway and its colonisation plan was inaugurated in 1970 by President Medici of Brazil. While teaching an ecology field class at Altamira, on the TransAmazon Highway, with environmental ecologist Robert Goodland, I began to realise how serious the issue of deforestation of tropical rainforest had become. We could see that much of the devastation was in vain, for projects that were unsustainable were being undertaken. For instance, unproductive land was being used as cattle pasture, but could support less than one cow per hectare over the eight-year lifetime of the field before it had to be abandoned altogether. Cattle farming was being sustained by a completely false economy of tax incentives and land speculation.

This first-hand experience of the futility of much of the deforestation led me gradually to change the emphasis of my research interests to a much more applied approach. I worked far more on economic botany and became concerned about some of the environmental problems related to the use of tropical rainforest. This involved both the search for new plants of possible economic use and the study of the ecology and land use systems of the Amazon Indians. I am sure that I was able to make this change in direction more easily because of my Christian faith and the consequent concern for justice and peace.

However, it was my faith that was strengthened from this experience because finally my botany and my faith came together; the dichotomy between work as a scientist and my church life had ended. The two began to strengthen and to complement each other in a new way rather than being separate compartments of my life. The biblical command of Genesis 2:15 to till and to keep (literally, to serve and preserve) the land began to take on a new meaning for me. I could add my own list of the wonders of creation to those of the psalmist who wrote Psalm 104, that wonderful hymn of creation.

As my interest in Christian ecology has grown under the guidance of the Holy Spirit, so has my sadness that the church has been slow to respond to this issue—the care of God's creation. The much quoted John 3:16 tells us that 'God so loved the cosmos that he gave his only begotten Son'. Colossians 1:15 reaffirms that the redeeming work of Christ was for more than the benefit of man, the one creature made in his image. Verse 17 says, 'He is before all things, and in him all things hold together' and verses 19 to 20: 'For it was the Father's good pleasure for all the fulness to dwell in him, and through him to reconcile all things to himself, having made peace through the blood of his cross; through him, I say, whether things on earth or things in heaven.' Those of us who are reconciled to God in Christ are also reconciled to his creation, and the only chance of survival for that creation is if those who are reconciled defend the creation. Today, many people look to New Age beliefs on which to base their environmental action. It is particulary important for those who know and worship the Creator rather than creation to be at the forefront of environmental protection.

Perhaps one of the common temptations for an environmentally concerned ethnobotanist, who has spent considerable time living among indigenous peoples, is to embrace the animist beliefs which often make them strong protectors of the environment. This is where the New Age movement would have us go.

On my first expedition to tropical rainforest I had an experience which I have never forgotten. After a long flight in a small plane to the remotest part of Suriname —two days by dugout canoe and two days on foot—we finally reached the base camp of the botanical expedition that I was to join for the next three months. After only a few minutes of exploration around the camp, I was excited to discover a flowering tree of the genus *Licania* on which I had worked for my doctoral thesis at Oxford. I asked the expedition leader, whom I had met for the first time thirty minutes previously, to arrange for the collection of herbarium specimens of the tree. He asked Frederick, our Suriname cook, to cut down the tree so that I could collect the samples. Our leader was quite annoyed when Frederick refused to fell the tree and an argument ensued. Frederick reluctantly agreed to fell the tree, but only after half an hour so that he would first have time to appease his deity, the 'bushy mama'. Later, after a time of ritual and prayer, Frederick cut the tree while chanting a song to the bushy mama blaming the white man for this unneccessary destruction. The tree fell and I excitedly gathered my collections from the flowering branches that were now on the ground. This incident is certainly the reason that I have preferred using tree climbers rather than the axe on my own expeditions. However, it is one of the many ways in which I have encountered nature protection in the religious beliefs of the rainforest dwellers. The forest is often under the care of much better protectors with the indigenous peoples than with the Western missionaries who replace their culture.

I have not fallen for the temptation of following the animist beliefs of the Indians because of the personal experience of my faith in Christ and the working of the Holy Spirit. My experience of such beliefs has led me to search the Scriptures more ardently for the many ways in which they teach a rich creation theology and thereby provide a firm basis for understanding the need to protect rather than destroy the earth. It has also led me to become involved in 'missionary earthkeeping'—using every opportunity to encourage missionaries to accept the Bible's teaching on caring for creation. It is vital that when the church sends out missionaries to remote areas, they are well versed in Christian ecology based on the principles of stewardship that are so explicit in the Scriptures. This is not only relevant to Christian work in the rainforest, but is also essential nearer to home.

However, when I attend one of the rare meetings of Christian ecologists (such as the annual gathering of the Au Sable Institute of Environmental Studies in Michigan), the common lament of the participants is that they are lone voices as defenders of creation in their home churches. This has certainly been my own experience, although it is encouraging for me to receive an increasing number of invitations from churches to speak on ecological issues. As I have become more involved in environmental issues, I have not just attempted to introduce more green issues into the churches, but rather, my research interests have been stimulated by my faith. The two aspects that have been most helpful are the study of creation and the Creator, and the biblical basis for justice and equity. It is no longer enough for me merely to classify and describe the plant species of the Amazon forest; I must also use my research data to address issues of deforestation, pollution, starvation and other problems that surround us today. I am a much more concerned person because my faith helps to remove more selfish motives.

I began this chapter with a childhood episode that might

have caused me to be against a strict observance of the Sabbath. However, the God-given principle of rest on the seventh day is part of a biblical ecology (Ex 23:10–11; Lev 25:1–13); it has also been one of the greatest strengths to my career. Since accepting Christ at Oxford, I have always used Sunday as a day of rest and worship, and have never done any work on Sunday unless on an expedition where the programme must continue regardless of the day of the week. I am where I am today because I am a workaholic who has always worked long hard hours. But this has never extended to Sunday; the Creator knew what he was doing when he rested on the seventh day.

As I have studied indigenous agricultural systems, I have come increasingly to appreciate the need for land as well as humans to rest, and the wisdom of the biblical principle of fallow. It is significant that the principle of fallow in Exodus 23:10–11 is also 'that the poor of your people may eat; and what they leave the wild beasts may eat'. This is another example of the richness of biblical ecology that we need to appreciate in the church today as we face the green movement and New Age beliefs. A scientist is often under great pressure to work solidly seven days a week. Enthusiasm for a research project can easily lead one into a seven-day week. The fact that this has never been a possibility in my mind has been a great strength to me and has helped both my work and my faith.

Recently, the Brazilian Minister for the Environment echoed the words of Lynn White, in his 1967 paper, that blamed Christianity for the current ecological crisis. The Minister said in March 1990, 'Christianity is at the root of the destruction of nature and the rainforest. Once you invent a god separate from nature, nature does not matter any more. It's something to use as you please. The Hindus, the Buddhists, saw nature as perfect and tried to harmonise with it.' The challenge for the future is to set this record straight and to show that those who know the Creator through a relationship with his Son, Jesus Christ, also become the stewards of the creation with which we have been entrusted. This will make the work of the Christian ecologist all the more of a challenge in the future.

6

Non in tempore sed cum tempore

Robert Boyd – Space scientist

Sir Robert L.F. Boyd, CBE, PhD, FIEE, F Inst Phys, FRAS, FRS.
Born 1922. Educated Whitgift School and Imperial College, London.
Professor of Physics, University College, London, 1962–83.
Director, Mullard Space Science Laboratory, University College, London, 1965–83.
Professor of Astronomy, Royal Institution, 1961–67.
Bakerian Lecturer of the Royal Society, 1978.
President, Victoria Institute, 1965–76.
Chairman, London Bible College, 1983–90.
Trustee, National Maritime Museum, 1980–89.
Governor, St Lawrence College, Ramsgate, 1965–76.
Governor, Southlands College, Wimbledon.

St Augustine's insight, that the whole of time and space and everything in them is God's giving, encapsulates, on the side of physics, my understanding of the relationship of God to the world of my professional study. At the more personal level, Christ's reply to his disciple Philip, 'He that has seen me has seen the Father', captures the essence of my faith. Of course, I did not see things like this as a child, but, having had a father who was both a Christian and a scientist, I grew up with a sense of the importance of *both* ways of thinking without the tensions between them that all too easily make teenagers (and others) embrace one or other view to the exclusion of its complement.

I graduated in electrical engineering from Imperial College during the war, having realised after the first year at college that I should have read physics. However, I persuaded the Admiralty, on being recruited to my war-time job, to treat me as a physicist and found myself associated with Professor (later Sir) Harrie Massey and D.R. (later Sir David) Bates; when the war ended, I was appointed as a research assistant in Massey's department (Mathematics) at University College, London (UCL), and moved with him to the Department of Physics. In 1953, at Massey's suggestion, I started a pioneering activity in Australia to use rockets at Woomera in high altitude studies and, with the advent of artificial satellites, became involved in the proposals for and instrumentation of the UK's Ariel 1 satellite.

We had good success and soon found we needed more laboratory space to be able to take up the many oppor-tunities that came our way. Again at Massey's suggestion, I started to look for a vacant stately home and funds to acquire it. In 1965, my group of about eighty workers moved into Holmbury House outside the village of Holmbury St Mary, and for the next few years we provided instrumentation for a new spacecraft at an average rate of about one a year, mostly for the study of solar system plasmas and for X-ray astronomy. During this time many of the duties, privileges and honours that accompany univer-sity workers who get in on the ground floor in this kind of work came my way. Increasingly, I was able to play a role in establishing policy—a task with which I am still involved although retired from my Chair. It is a great pleasure to me that my present activities, as a Fellow of the Royal Society, involve me in the use of spacecraft to respond to the responsibility and challenge of the study and care of our global environment.

I have always been sad at the way the predominantly arts graduates in the media represent our Christian faith as outmoded by science, whereas I have not found this attitude among most senior scientists. So, when I moved into the house of the Director of Mullard Space Science Laboratory at Holmbury St Mary (which, although I named it after the principal benefactor, was still a part of the Department of Physics and Astronomy of UCL), I thought it would be a good idea if I used the Christmas issue of St Mary's parish magazine to let the village know that the head of the somewhat mysterious laboratory at the top of the hill was not at all like the 'mad' scientist of tradition but a grateful and dependent disciple of Christ, as were many of his colleagues. I did this by writing some verses relating aspects of science I was particularly interested in to my faith. They are entitled 'Creation', and I do not think I can do better than quote them here.

> 'In the beginning', long before all worlds
>   Or flaming stars or whirling galaxies,
> Before that first 'big bang', if such it was,
>   Or earlier contraction: back and back
> Beyond all time or co-related space
>   And all that is and all that ever was
> And all that yet will be; Source of the whole,
>   'In the beginning was the Word' of God.

> The Word of God; Reason, Design and Form,
>   Intelligence, Whose workshop spans the stars,
> Expressed within the Cosmos and alike
>   In what seems chaos; He Who works as much
> In randomness as order, Who to make
>   Man in His image scorns not to create
> By patient evolution on a scale
>   Of craft divine which dwarfs a million years.

> Who is this God, that bows Himself to see
>   The puny wonders of this little speck
> Of cosmic dust that we have named our Earth,
>   The toy volcanoes and the restless sea

That splashes from His bucket like a drop
   And still a captive to the circling Moon
Flows and recedes, purging polluted shores
   Or sending tidal torrents up the Severn?

Who is this God, that circles either pole
   With fluorescent light, an arctic dawn,
Whose rain makes little sparks and tiny cracks
   That we call thunder storms, this God Whose plan
So shapes the atoms that they must combine
   To give dust life and then to feed that dust
With inorganic substance to create
   By DNA a pattern like its own?

Who is this God and can this God be known
   Within the confines of a human skull,
A litre and a half of mortal brain
   Whose interlinking neurons must depend
On chemistry and physics in the end
   For all that man can know or comprehend?
Can man know God eternally enthroned
   Throughout all space and in the great beyond?

The mystery of being, still unsolved
   By all our science and philosophy,
Fills me with breathless wonder, and the God
   From Whom it all continually proceeds
Calls forth my worship and shall worship have.
   But love in incarnation draws my soul
To humble adoration of a Babe;
   'In this was manifest the love of God.'

Still Jesus comes to those who seek for God
   And still He answers as He did of old,
'I've been with you so long, how can you say
   "I don't know God, oh show me God today"?
When you've met Me you've seen the eternal God,
   Met Him as Father too, as He who cares
And loves and longs for men as I myself.
   I am the Christmas message. God has come.'

It will be evident that in 1972, when I wrote these verses, as now, I find the idea of God beyond and wholly other than his universe as the 'Giver of the whole show' to be basic. Like many of my generation, I owe both that phrase and this clarification of my thinking largely to the late Professor Donald MacKay. The crystallisation of the concept of Christ (rather than the Bible) as the basic datum of my faith I owe to Dr Oliver Barclay and the little (at that time) group of Christian research scientists that he got together and led in the early fifties. In this no book played a greater part than Carnegie Simpson's *The Fact of Christ*. The establishment of a close and worshipful personal relationship with God the Father and his Son is probably mostly due to my parents and the Christians with whom they worshipped.

I only write poetry when I feel deeply, so each verse above says something about my thinking. I suppose the most obvious thing is my biblical references. Early in my professional life I was uneasy about the mutual incompatability of biblical accounts of the same event, if taken as literal statements—the impossibility of a complete harmony of the Gospels would be a case in point. Equally, the divergence between literal biblical accounts and the evidence of science presented a problem to me at that time. The notorious 'omphalos' question was, as the word implies, the crux of the matter. Did Adam have a navel or not? (Did the trees in the Garden of Eden have rings?) If 'no' he was not a man like us; if 'yes' there appeared to be evidence of a past history that had not happened.

As I gradually came, by my regular attention to it, to hear Holy Scripture (or should I say God in it?) actually addressing my situation, morally, wisely and graciously, I realised that the Godhead who emptied himself ('kenosis') to be incarnate in Jesus also stooped to speak in our colloquial idiom and through imperfect human personalities. The *Logos* was dynamic in Scripture and in nature as well as in Christ. So the first verse and a half of my poem reflect the opening verses of St John's Gospel and relate the Jesus of my faith to the cosmos of my studies. Especially significant are the words 'as much in randomness as order', for the Giver of the whole must surely be no denizen of space and time but in his otherness (no pantheism for me!) be the Giver of those very processes that to my limited set of 'interlinking neurones' are random. The God who in Christ so perfectly addresses and meets my ethical and numinous needs is, in that interaction, far too intimate to be a mere deistic clockmaker, blind or otherwise.

The words 'Whose workshop spans the stars' owe something to a stimulating remark made by Dr John Hercus of Sydney. 'Robert,' he said, 'has it ever occurred to you that God probably had to make a universe as large as ours to be able to evolve man?' That was decades ago. Modern cosmology tinted, if not actually coloured by the anthropic principle, is increasingly accepting this with or without its theistic overtones. This verse also reflects the insight so many of us gained from Donald MacKay and his inveighing against 'nothing buttery'. That which I study in the world of physics, seen from another angle, is the handiwork of God. The processes of science are the techniques of Deity— 'Stormy wind fulfilling his word'. Verse three makes the point that physical size is not the divine criterion of importance or value, a fact that was not lost on the writer of Isaiah 40. It is also tinged, as in the fourth verse, with my own interest in astronomy and in terrestrial phenomena— volcanoes, the Severn bore, the aurora, lightning and the origin of life.

It has often seemed to me that, as scientists, we are in danger of becoming intoxicated with the success of our own thinking (verse five) and so we fail to recognise the inevitable limitation of the finite computing structure that constitutes our minds. If, as now seems to be an exciting possibility, in the context of physical processes the universe may be seen as the result of a quantum fluctuation in the 'vacuum' (whatever that may be), only the most myopic

would say that the whole of human experience and achievement on 'this little speck of cosmic dust' is adequately
described as 'nothing but' the outcome of such a fluctuation.
The last two verses speak for themselves and conjoin my
thinking as scientist and amateur theologian to what is vital
to any personal knowledge of God—encounter. I cannot
say when I first had this encounter, but that it becomes
increasingly real and vital to me with the passage of time I
am in no doubt.

The problem of suffering

As I look back on my life as a Christian believer I am aware
that my verses fail to address a crucial problem of faith for
me and perhaps for many. I become more and more aware
of the problem of suffering as my vision of the world has
become less science centred. I never took the naïve attitude
that seems, in these days, to characterise many immature
Christians, where prayer is thought of as a way of persuad-
ing God to smooth one's path. To stand (literally) at
Gethsemane was enough to confirm in me the recognition
that the way of Christ is the way of the cross. But I have
increasingly come to understand that 'nature red in tooth
and claw' cannot, to mix the metaphors, be 'swept under
the carpet'. The poem I quoted above was originally
entitled 'Christmas' and caught some of the calm joy of
Emmanuel, but earlier, after being very moved by a
Passion play presented at St Lawrence College, Ramsgate,
of which I was a governor, I wrote verses entitled 'Easter'.
In so far as I have found a resolution to the problem of
suffering, it is not in rational comprehension but in divine
empathy and, in my experience, that is what the sufferer
needs.

The verses that follow do not avoid the reality of
suffering; rather, they trace some of it to its true source in
sin, but only some. They are subtitled 'The glory that

should follow', a quotation from 1 Peter 1:11 That they are
a commentary on Philippians 2 is obvious.

'Highly exalted', this the unsought prize
    Of your humiliation and your pain.
Equality with God was, in your eyes,
    Not to be grasped but unity with man.

The form of deity was on this Earth
    Only in you, the emptied servant, seen.
And form of servitude, with Godlike worth,
    In no one else but you has ever been.

One, only one has full obedience shown,
    Of all the myriad sons to mothers born.
Obedience such as yours deserves a crown.
    O Jesus 'twas a diadem of thorn!

That chaplet which they thrust upon your brow
    Was of my weaving, and that anguish sore,
Though of your choosing, from such seeds did grow
    Which I had sown. For me the nails you bore.

Still as my memory frames that scene of woe
    My mind recoils where you my Lord stood fast.
I wince to hear the hammer's fearful blow:
    Occasion of forgiveness unsurpassed.

Blinded by tears I see unconquered love,
    Stretched in the awful tension of the tree,
Refuse the scornful challenge to remove
    And choose to stay transfixed there for me.

I know the grace that brought my Saviour down
    From Godhead wealth to naked poverty,
That bought for me the riches of a crown
    At the unmeasured cost of Calvary.

Jesus what kind of joy could you foresee
    That made you think so lightly of the shame,
Endure the nameless terrors of the tree,
    In tortured darkness carry all my blame?

This is the nature of your love divine,
    Eternal, self-creating, of such worth
That it could find a joy in seeking mine
    T'outweigh the fearful cost of such a death.

Your love has won. You are the conqueror now.
    A name beyond all other names is yours.
O blessed Jesus, at your name I bow
    And worship you with all created powers.

I see you now exalted to the throne
    Of God Himself, My greatest joy is this
That you are there; the Lamb of God once slain
    Source and circumference of heaven's bliss.

The problem of natural disasters (and others) remains, perhaps even more insistently than that of 'nature red in tooth and claw'. It is all too easy for the physicist and astronomer impressed with the grandeur of the cosmos to overlook it. I sympathise with the pressure of this problem on my biological colleagues. But if there is statistical evidence for theistic faith being more widespread among physical scientists than life scientists, as some claim, I wonder if the unhappy 'either or', rather than 'both and' conflict between science and faith that arose over evolution in the last century is not really responsible.

I offer no logical resolution of the problem any more than I can resolve the 'mystery of being'. I can only say that the whole of modern physics on the one hand and of the revelation of God in Christ on the other seem both so utterly unpredictable, unexpected and transcendental to material reality as we experience it directly, that I have long since ceased to respect any philosophy that seeks to decide ultimate questions (after the manner of the Greeks) by the power of unfettered thought. In faith, as in science, I am essentially an empiricist. The only sense I can make of the Phenomenon-of-Christ is still, as his converted opponent St Paul wrote long ago, 'God was in Christ reconciling the world to himself' (2 Cor 5:19). To set forward the experience of that reconciliation is still a task in which I would want to participate. But, as the same apostle wrote earlier to the same leaders, 'The message of the cross is to those who are perishing, foolishness; but to us who are being saved it is the power of God' (1 Cor 1:18). I do not find this surprising. One only has to look around, not to say within, to see the tragedy of the daily perishing of the pristine humanity of many of our fellows and to recognise within the daily need of a saving power beyond ourselves.

7

Biology and Belief

Andrew Miller – Molecular biologist

Professor Andrew Miller, MA, BSc, PhD, FRSE.
Born 1936. Educated Beath High School and Edinburgh University.
Principal and Vice-Chancellor, University of Sterling since 1994.
Professor of Biochemistry at Edinburgh University 1984–94, seconded as Director of Research, European Synchrotron Radiation Facility, Grenoble, France.
Formerly at Medical Research Council Molecular Biology Laboratory, Cambridge and Lecturer in Molecular Biophysics, University of Oxford.
Head of the European Molecular Biology Laboratory, Grenoble, France.

The area of science in which I work is variously called biophysics, biochemisty or molecular biology. It is the application of the methods of physics and chemistry to living things in order to find out how they work. We want to explain the function of living things in terms of the atoms and molecules of which they are composed.

The last thirty years have seen dramatic progress in molecular biology. The first half of the twentieth century saw revolutionary changes at the foundations of physics in relativity theory and quantum mechanics. The second half of our century is likely to be remembered for the transformation in biological sciences. This has completely modified both our understanding of living things and our ability to control or manipulate them. My aim in this chapter is to give a brief account of this progress and to discuss some implications.

When Einstein formulated his theories of special and general relativity, their impact on the popular mind was that they implied a radical revision in our view of the world. Much more radical, however, was the nature of the quantum mechanics revolution in our mode of thought, since it seemed to indicate that quantum events were uncaused, and even now extensive debate is taking place on its significance for our thinking. While the revolution in biological science is perhaps not so profound conceptually as those in physics, the impact on our perception of ourselves is likely to be just as great.

In all living organisms there are three kinds of large molecules or macromolecules with molecular weights ranging from thousands to millions. These are the proteins, the nucleic acids and the polysaccharides; I will discuss the first two. Each of these three macromolecular types are long chain polymers composed of linear strings of smaller molecules called monomers, which act as subunits. These molecules all consist of only a few different chemical elements— carbon, hydrogen, oxygen, nitrogen and phosphorus and somewhat less of several other elements.

Proteins are the molecules which make up the bodies of animals. Muscle, skin and tendons, ligaments, hair and feathers are all proteins. Proteins also are the molecules which make biological catalysts called enzymes. The enzymes are crucial biological macromolecules which enable chemical reactions which would normally require high temperatures or long times to occur rapidly at body temperatures. Other proteins have different but very important functions of transport, control and regulation of reactions, conversion of chemical energy to mechanical work or conversion of energy in light to chemical energy.

Proteins are polymers of amino-acids. There are some twenty different kinds of amino-acids with differing size and electrical properties. It is the order in which these different amino-acids occur along the protein chain which defines first how the protein molecule folds up to form a well defined three-dimensional structure and second, how that well defined structure is able to perform the specific function—enzyme, transport, light-harvesting, etc—of the protein in the organism.

Let us take a specific protein, an enzyme called lysozyme, as an example. Lysozyme occurs in human tears where it acts as a mild antiseptic by catalysing the breakdown of the molecules which make up the protective outer coat of certain bacteria. All molecules of lysozyme (apart from genetic variations—more about this later) are exactly the same size, contain the same array of amino-acids in the same order along the protein chain, and this chain always folds up into precisely the same three-dimensional structure. By applying the rather complex technique of X-ray crystallography to crystals of lysozyme, this precise three-dimensional structure was worked out and represented by a molecular model which shows the positions of atoms in space. This model in turn reveals how the enzyme is able to carry out its function of attacking the bacterial walls. In general, enzyme structures contain a binding site, usually a cleft in the structure, which recognises the substrate by a snug geometrical fit. Once enzyme and substrate are fitted together, a so-called active site in the enzyme is brought into close proximity to the chemical bonds to be broken in the substrate and the fission can take place. Any influence which alters the structure of the protein usually results in loss of protein function, and this is readily understood since the precise geometrical fit of recognition is no longer possible. This also explains why an enzyme can be very selective in what it attacks.

By the time of writing, the structures of around 300 different proteins have been determined by X-ray crystallography, and once these structures are known they immediately suggest mechanisms whereby the proteins carry out their function. We now have well developed mechanims for how haemoglobin and myoglobin control the oxygen level in blood and in muscles respectively, how a large number of different enzymes perform their variety of catalytic functions, how sunlight is harvested in plant leaves by the reaction centre complex, how chlorophyl works, how antibodies recognise foreign materials in human plasma and how vaccines inactivate viruses. A whole new subject called structural molecular biology has blossomed and is currently expanding at a very fast rate. Structural molecular biology shows that living things function at the molecular level by a precise geometrical positioning in space and a high degree of synchronisation in time. This accuracy of positioning in space and time is crucial for a single event like enzyme action, but within the cells of plants and animals millions of such events must further be orchestrated in space and time so that the whole cell functions properly, and of course the cell also plays a defined role in a specific tissue (liver, brain, muscle, etc) which in turn has its specific role in the organism.

In summary, we are now beginning to see how the variety and specificity of all living things is fundamentally dependent on molecular recognition. Below the level of molecules, the atoms of living things are the same as the atoms of the inorganic world. In the biological molecules, however, there occur three-dimensional arrangements of atoms that are highly specific and allow molecular recognition to take place. The cells of living things then appear as vast assemblies of inter-related and interacting three-dimensional jigsaws which result in delicately controlled functions of the cell. This cellular function integrates with the function of millions of other cells, also under molecular control, to serve the overall function of the organism.

How do living organisms construct proteins with such precise structure? The answer lies in a second set of biological macromolecules, the nucleic acids. The nucleic acids are polymers in which the monomers are four different kinds of nucleotide. The function of the nucleic acids is principally to store and transmit information. They therefore make up the genes which are passed on through generations of organisms. There are two kinds of nucleic acid—deoxyribonucleic acid (DNA) and ribonucleic acid (RNA). The four kinds of nucleotides in DNA are adenine (A), thymine (T), guanine (G) and cytosine (C). In RNA, T is replaced by uracil (U).

In 1953, Crick and Watson made the key discovery by X-ray diffraction that the structure of DNA was a double helix. Two DNA chains are wound around each other rather like two strands of a two-strand rope. However, the crucial feature of the DNA double helix is the relation between the nucleotides in one strand and those in the other. In the central core of the double helix where the two strands touch, the A nucleotide of one strand pairs with the T nucleotide of the other, while the C nucleotide of one strand pairs with the G nucleotide of the other. So, if in one strand the order of the nucleotides was

C G T C A T G A T   then the other strand would
| | | | | | | | |
be   G C A G T A C T A

Crick and Watson wrote the memorable words. 'This immediately suggests a copying mechanism for the genetic material.' For if the double helix unwound, each of the two separate strands could coil a second chain around itself to form two double helices, each with the same order of nucleotides as in the parent double helix. And the mechanism whereby A only pairs with T, and C only pairs with G is again molecular recognition. More precisely, the distribution in space of the atoms in A and T allowed them to pair by forming internucleotide hydrogen bonds in a way that was impossible between A and C, A and G, T and C or T and G. Only A—T and C—G pairs are geometrically feasible except for some rare cases. Molecular recognition is thus the basis of the mechanism whereby genes of parents may be copied into genes of offspring.

This, of course, does not yet explain how proteins are formed. By the early 1960s the steps in protein synthesis became clear. Double helical DNA unwinds and is copied into complementary strands of RNA. (In DNA, A, T, C and G produce in RNA U, A, G and C, respectively.) Then the order of nucleotides in the RNA is scanned by cellular organelles called ribosomes. The RNA nucleotides are read three at a time and each triplet corresponds to one specific amino-acid which a messenger molecule brings to the ribosome and adds on to the growing protein chain. The 'dictionary' which relates triplets to amino-acids is called the genetic code. For example, if UUC occurs in the RNA, the amino-acid serine is added to the protein, or if GCA occurs in the RNA then alanine is the added amino-acid. The twenty different amino-acids each have their own triplet coding for them (with quite a generous redundancy since four different nucleotides taken three at a time yield sixty-four different triplets which is more than enough to define the twenty amino-acids that occur in the body; some amino-acids can be produced by up to four different triplets).

So let us summarise again. The order of nucleotides in the DNA (the genes) can be copied from generation to generation (with high though not precise fidelity and with complex mixing particularly in organisms which reproduce sexually). This order of nucleotides in DNA determines the order of nucleotides in complementary RNA which, in turn, defines the order of aminio-acids in the protein chain. This, in turn, determines the way in which the protein folds up into a well defined three-dimensional structure and this structure gives the protein its ability to function.

Incidentally, the unwinding and rebuilding of DNA as well as the reading of RNA all require specific enzymes which, of course, are proteins. This raises the question 'What came first: proteins (enzymes) or nucleic acids?' The discovery of a type of RNA with apparent enzyme activity, called ribosymes, suggests that nucleic acids came first.

With this general background we can now interpret many well known but previously incomprehensible features of biology and medicine.

On a personal note, I cannot forget the day in Oxford when my research group discovered a curious periodicity in the amino-acid sequence of the collagen molecule which immediately explained how molecular recognition between collagen molecules leads them to self-assemble into fibres of tendon. Collagen is the most abundant protein in mammals, accounting for one-third of human protein. It makes up tendons, skin, cartilege, cornea of the eye, the filtration system of the kidneys and the organic component of bone. The molecules are over 1,000 amino-acids long and have a triple helical structure. We could trace an unbroken set of causal links from gene (DNA) through RNA, protein sequences, protein helical structure, molecular assembly into fibrils and fibril assembly into visible tendon fibres. It was also instantly clear that the important biological fibres such as muscle and keratin will assemble in an analogous way.

The DNA–RNA protein framework also suggests mechanisms for protein evolution and for the molecular origin of certain diseases. It has yielded a powerful tool for intervention and control in medicine and agriculture leading to the new subjects of molecular medicine and molecular agriculture.

As described above, the DNA double helix suggests the mechanism whereby genes are passed on through generations. In order to work adequately the copying mechanism must be of high fidelity. However, the fidelity is not 100 per cent; errors do creep in leading to alterations or mutations in the newly formed DNA, and hence altered amino-acid sequence in the proteins. When these mutations occur irregularly, and we do not know their exact cause, we call them 'random'. Sometimes these mutations produce proteins that are unable to form or to function and they are termed 'lethal' if the organism cannot survive. However, many mutations are neutral and it has been noted that the number of differences in amino-acids of proteins is clearly proportional to their 'evolutionary distance'. For example, the proteins cytochrome c from humans and primates are much more similar than those from humans and insects. It is possible by using the differences between the amino-acid sequences in proteins to construct evolutionary trees which correspond well with such trees constructed on the basis of fossil and other evidence. Thus we find the new wealth of information on protein structure fits in with general ideas of evolution and suggests a mechanism whereby evolution may occur. If a mutation happens to produce an enzyme which is more stable or more effective, then a reproductive advantage can be given to the bearer of that mutation and to its progeny. It should be said that this does not yet explain the increase in complexity which we seem to see in evolutionary history, but it throws a lot of light on one aspect of what is going on.

Mutations can also lead to genetic diseases, many of them the result of well recognised molecular defects which account for the manifestations of the disease. The best known historical example is perhaps the widespread incidence of haemophilia in Queen Victoria's descendants, though she did not have the disease herself.

In the last few years a dramatic new technique has been developed which enables new proteins to be rationally designed. The method is called site-specific mutagenesis and is carried out now in scores of biochemistry and molecular biology laboratories. If a protein structure is known, it is possible to inspect it and decide to design a new protein in which a specific amino-acid is selectively replaced by another chosen amino-acid. This is done to investigate the effect of this site-specific change on the protein. The new protein is made by isolating the gene which codes for the original protein then, by using synthetic short sections of nucleic acids, to produce a new DNA with a chosen altered nucleotide sequence. The new DNA is then incorporated into the 'gene' of a bacterial culture and the synthetic mechanism of the bacteria produces the new protein *in vitro*. In this way, proteins have been engineered with altered enzyme activity, with improved heat stability and with stronger antibody-antigen binding. The next few years will almost certainly see a wide range of specifically engineered proteins for industrial, agricultural and medical purposes. Bacteria will also be used to produce large quantities of valuable proteins which occur naturally only in tiny quantities. Unfortunately, while we are learning a lot about human (and plant and animal) genetics and the modification of genes in disease, we are not yet able to replace deleterious human genes so that they function normally, though it is not unreasonable to expect such developments in the next few decades.

A major project in molecular biology, the achievement of which will require international collaboration, is the determination of the nucleotide sequence of a human genome. The resulting information would be comparable in bulk with that in the *Encyclopaedia Britannica*. The scientific techniques required are available, though high quality management and co-ordination will be essential for the success of the project. It has also been suggested that systematic efforts be made to determine the structures of all the (available) proteins. The availability of such an encyclopedic natural history of biomolecular anatomy would provide a secure basis for the development of molecular medicine. However, rather more subtle and original probes of the driving forces and controls behind the molecular machinery will also be required.

Living beings

Of course, the account of molecular biology I have just given is grossly simplified and no proper idea is given of the immense range of biological problems which have been clarified. The reader interested in learning more is directed to the appropriate textbooks. However, I hope I have conveyed the general flavour of the profound revolution that is still taking place in our understanding of living things. A large number of difficult problems remain.

For example, we do not really understand the essence of living things—I mean scientifically, not philosophically. Organisms metabolise, reproduce and evolve. But why? Can life be explained fully in terms of physics and chemistry? The most direct approach to this central question has been taken by Manfred Eigen. The complex structure and functioning of proteins, nucleic acids and other molecules is fascinating and will produce a very powerful tool for manipulating the biological world. But what is the rationale of the whole interlocking show we call 'life'? Living things behave, as we say, with a lif of their own. James Lovelock has even suggested that the entire biosphere on earth seems to act as a self-controlling unity he has called Gaia. Eigen is trying to analyse living systems in terms of hypercycles. Hypercycles are cyclical sequences of linked reactions in which the products of one reaction act as reactants for the next. Such cycles are familiar to biochemists who have established the existence of metabolic cycles and chains of reactions in organs such as liver and muscle. These metabolic cycles are mechanisms whereby we extract chemical energy from food and use it to construct essential molecular components in specialised organs of the body. Metabolic cycles are similar over a wide range of organisms but there are also striking differences. Eigen's hypercycle idea is broader than that of metabolic cycles. He is analysing the physico-chemical self-establishment and stability of these hypercycles and seeing if the computer-generated simulated behaviour of such cycles corresponds at all with how living things actually behave. The aim is to see if the apparent self-determination and goal orientation of organisms can be accounted for fully by physics and chemistry. Molecular biology will always be more than just physics and chemistry—there will be essential boundary conditions. Contingency will be evident.

Yet another approach is to ask whether or not some recent ideas on the properties of so-called chaotic systems are relevant to biology. In some systems it is well known that order can arise from disorder in a spontaneous fashion. These systems are not running contrary to the second law of thermodynamics since they are open systems with energy input. Crystal formation from solution is a simple example of such a system, but there are many other examples with a wide range of complexity. Some interesting principles emerge of how chaotic or disordered systems could spontaneously produce order. Could living cells be special cases of these principles? Perhaps living cells are not so dependent on the vagaries of history in evolution but represent the best stable assemblies of matter quite apart from natural selection which, of course, may still have a role to play.

So the new subject of biotechnology has recently appeared. To be more precise, biotechnology has recently burgeoned since we have had traditional biotechnologies of cooking, brewing, dyeing, and so on for millenia. But molecular biology is leading to a revolution in biotechnology. This practical success is raising serious problems in how to cope with it—economic, administrative, legal and ethical. But we should be clear that we still do not know how life arose, or what the explanation is of the extraordinary stability coupled with fragility and plasticity of the biosphere. There remain major problems, such as how cells differentiate, how the forms of organisms develop, what cancer involves, and so on, which seem extremely difficult but probably tractable. Over all hangs the problem of consciousness.

Belief in God

There are several points mentioned above at which the emerging structural biology impinges on the Christian faith, but here I will discuss only one—belief in God. Although some of the picture I have sketched is fairly new, the general pattern has been evident since the early 1960s and has been commented upon by some of the scientists who created the picture—Monod, Crick, Jacob, Lwoff, Medawar and by skilful writers such as Richard Dawkins, Stephen Gould and Peter Atkins. Several of these writers conclude that theism is no longer tenable in the light of recent discoveries in biology. It is not possible to discuss all the arguments presented but I will try to give the main drift.

Dawkins says that before 1859 it was reasonable to believe in God because there was no other convincing explanation of the complexity of living things. After 1859, natural selection provided the explanation so (although, as the blurb on the cover of Dawkin's *Blind Watchmaker* says, there may be other reasons for belief in God) biological complexity is no longer a good reason for theism. He quotes Paley's well known argument of the watch as evidence for the design in the living world.

The argument from design ('There is design so there must be a designer') and its relative, the cosmological argument ('The fact that there exists something rather than nothing requires an explanation'), have a long history. The argument from design was used in the New Testament by Paul to the Romans '[God's] invisible attributes ... have been visible to the eye of reason, in the things that He has made' (Rom 1:20). The same argument was known to the pre-Christian Cicero who rejected it, but it was taken up in the second century AD by Tertullian on the Christian side. Varieties of the argument from design in the physical world to a Creator were used by most natural philosophers (the term 'scientist' was not used until 1834) up to the middle of the nineteenth century.

Then, in the nineteenth and early twentieth centuries, several influential thinkers explained God away. Durkeim pronounced God as a projection of society as a whole. Freud maintained that God was a projection of the father figure and that religion was a collective neurosis of society, while Marx held that religion, an ideology to bolster a type of production economy, was the opium of the people. Feurbach said that God was the product of wishful thinking and Nietzsche proclaimed the death of God. The Tubingen theologian Strauss applied historical analysis to the New Testament and wrote a *Life of Christ* which was supposed to abolish Christianity within a generation (of 1835). Of course, so many different explanations for God was clearly overkill. As a whole, though they contributed to the eventual secularisation of society, they were not widely convincing and more than a century later a professionally conducted opinion poll in the UK (December 1989) found 70 per cent of adults claiming to believe in God. Over the same century dramatic changes have taken place in psychology, sociology, Marxism, history and New Testament criticism. The real damage to theism was supposed to have been done by Hume in the eighteenth century. He argued that all perceptions of the human mind are either impressions of experience or ideas; whereas the relations between ideas can be known with certainty, the facts of reality cannot be established. Belief in the natural world (though a practical necessity) and in the existence of God, cannot be proved by reason. The problem there is that Hume's apparently cogent argument also implied that science should not work either. Philosophy is not always a sound guide to reality.

It is important to be clear that although the work of eighteenth- and nineteenth-century thinkers were strong influences, leading to the secularisation of a Christendom which had lasted for 1,500 years, the design argument for theism was much wider than Paley's example of order in the biological world. The design argument lay in considering the basic regularities in nature and reflecting on their origin and implications. Paley's arguments from biology were a special case of this wider argument. Paley's argument is now unconvincing since it involves details of mechanism within the universe; he brought in a 'God of the gaps' to explain gaps in our understanding—a God who therefore shrinks with our increase in knowledge. The original design argument is really untouched by Darwin since it was based on regularities in the whole of physical science as well as biology. When we try to clearly indicate the difference between theism and atheism the fundamental question is whether or not the universe has a purpose. Does the universe have a personal Creator and hence a purpose or is it entirely the result of mindless forces?

The fact that we are here obviously means that there has been a bringing into being, a creation. Leibnitz' question 'Why is there something rather than nothing?' calls for an explanation of creation, and cosmologists are actively engaged in trying to provide one. Scientific theories which involve the creation of matter out of nothing have been proposed and some (apparently at present) have been falsified. At present, some cosmologists are looking for a theory of everything (TOE) which, from several basic principles, will explain the emergence of the universe and the present distribution of matter within it. Some theories even imply a sort of natural selection between possible universes. These cosmologists have not yet succeeded so, as in the case of biology before 1859, it would still be possible, following Dawkins' logic, on present scientific knowledge to say, 'It could be God.' But this would be the 'God of the gaps' of Paley's argument. The real reason that leads to belief in God is more fundamental than our inability to see how things work or how they came about.

Let us take the case of gravitation. The laws of gravitation, together with those of dynamics, are adequate to explain with considerable precision the movements of the celestial bodies and of lunar and solar system probes sent from earth. The fact that we can predict accurately the behaviour of gravitational and inertial masses in no way rules out a purposive God as the Creator of these laws. Christians (and others) see the activity of God in the parts we understand as well as those that we do not. God is the ground of our being. We may know the laws of physics which allow us to calculate and often predict events in nature, but it is not the laws of physics which make events happen. These laws describe the events and their regularities. God is the Author, the Creator in the usual terms, of the world. It is very difficult to decide whether or not observed order originates from personal purpose or not. Purpose involves the idea of intentionality. Was such and such consciously planned or the result of unconscious forces?

Monod got close to the heart of the debate in a book published in French in 1970, and in English as *Chance and Necessity* in 1972, when he contrasted what he called animist religions with the secular, objective view of the world. However, it is wrong to classify Christianity as animism. A.N. Whitehead, H. Butterfield, R. Hookyaas and others have pointed out that a key development of Christian thought beyond earlier Greek ideas was the de-deification of nature, a development which, it has plausibly been argued, provided the appropriate intellectual environment for the development of modern science. In Christianity, the Creator and his creation are quite distinct. The creation is not worshipped and may be investigated, as Francis Bacon put it in the seventeenth century, 'For the relief of man's estate'. In fact, this very concept has been suggested as the root cause of the thoughtless exploitation of nature and of our present environmental crisis. Exploitation, however, is not a Christian concept, for the idea of man's stewardship under God is the dominant feature of the biblical attitude towards the natural world—a view that today could be described as being as green as you can get.

However, in spite of our awareness that the Paley

arguments taken by themselves are no longer convincing, some reflection on what we know about the route by which life developed shows it to be so remarkable that there seems to be more to it than just physical chemistry. Let me say immediately that I am not thinking of vital forces. I am not saying that because I can't see how it came about, it must be God. How I wish some writers, once they have got over the excitement of what we know, would be just as open about the vast areas of puzzlement and ignorance which still exist in biology. It is flying well ahead of the evidence and counter to much of experience in the history of science to say that we know that it is all going to be explained by our present-day concepts. It is worth recalling that James Clerk Maxwell, perhaps the greatest nineteenth-century physicist, said in 1872 that 'The ether is the largest and most evident body of which we have knowledge'. Within some twenty-five years the ether no longer 'existed'. Young scientists are motivated by the challenge of the great unknown and it is not productive to forget this.

When we think of the host of coincidences which had to occur to produce life, even once the Big Bang was safely over, they are remarkable. The relative sizes of the moon and the earth are, as far as we know, unique, with the implication that monthly regularities are imposed on the earth in a way that almost certainly was essential to get the rhythm of life going. Our moon is the right size to set up a joint system with the earth which produces a terrestial magnetic core with properties which favoured the development of life.

I have no space to describe further the 'luck' which this earth has enjoyed to allow life to develop, but it is so remarkable that either one says 'Well, it has happened so a physical explanation is all we need look for', a sort of atheism based on personal credulity, or to admit that it might reflect an underlying purpose. To say that natural selection is an anti-random device, a pattern generator, or a probability augmentor, is close to vital force sort of obfuscation. Natural selection can be shown to produce order in a comprehensible way on a very modest scale indeed, and to extrapolate to the whole show is clearly wishful thinking, and not scientific. Of course, scientists must back their hunches, but it is important to be open and perceptive of the situation. It has been said, correctly, that at present we are not in a position to know whether the development of life was inevitable (ie, highly probable) or a lucky accident (highly improbable). It is difficult to be more uncertain.

But biology does not stand on its own. In contrast to the writings of the biologists mentioned above, physical scientists writing on their subject often naturally use the word 'God'. I am thinking of Hawking, Davies, Polkinghorne, Freeman-Dyson, Squires, Josephson, Cottrell, Lovell, Pippard and Coulson. We cannot write off scientists of this calibre as a loony fringe any more than we can the biologists.

All of these physicists except Hawking, who is ambivalent, appear to believe in God; but this is not the point I wish to make here. My point is that they deal in concepts analogous to those of theism. Analysis of modern physical theory shows that ideas based on our everyday experience are not trusty guides to all parts of the physical world. The key criterion in physical theory, as in theism, is empirical testing: 'Seek and you shall find'; 'Taste and see that the Lord is gracious.' Our ideas must be regulated by reality and not vice-versa. Some biologists tend to be so impressed by the success of a particular idea that they become intoxicated and see it as the global answer to everything. Gould's stimulating *Wonderful Life* is a bit like this. He is thrilled at the totally different species which occur among the fossils of the Burgess Shale. He decided, with rather little quantitative evaluation and contrary to the conclusions of other paleontologists, that there is a greater diversity of species in the Burgess Shale than in these phyla now. He then magnifies this idea up to a revolutionary new insight into the nature of life and the meaning of existence. He wildly theorises on the result of rewinding and playing back a recording of evolutionary development and he discovers that contingency is a concept that is needed. This is heady stuff, with full marks for enthusiasm and originality, characteristics much needed these days. However, careful critical testing will have to be carried out in order to separate the durable from the ephemeral. In the meantime, we wait and see.

Furthermore, there remains consciousness, the great mystery of biology which strongly suggests that surprises are in store for future scientists. Many new concepts are offered to help understand the phenomenon of consciousness, including the notion that we should not talk about it at all in scientific discussions. In fact, we do not have a theory of consciousness. There is no need to invoke the God of the gaps here or even to think we are forced to a mind/body dualism. My own view is that we will build up a natural history of consciousness. We will learn what kinds of electronic circuitry in the neurones can result in consciousness and which ones cannot. Obviously, it will not be easy technically to get this sort of information, and even more difficult (perhaps impossible) to set up falsifiable or verifiable tests for consciousness. Assuming these problems could be overcome, consciousness would take on the same status as gravity, inertial force or magnetism. It might even be possible to think of a theory which 'explained' consciousness in terms of dynamic electronic circuitry.

Recently, it has been emphasised that determinate physical systems can readily develop into chaotic systems where predictability is no longer possible. The development of weather patterns is an example of this. It has been suggested that this kind of indeterminacy may allow the intervention of a Creator or a Mind to nudge physical systems in the direction of the Creators's or the Mind's will. This is too close to a God (or a Mind) of the gaps for my liking. At present there is no theory that even approaches the problem of the relation between mind and matter. Roger Penrose, a leading theoretical physicist, has recently published *The Emperor's New Clothes*, a superb account of present-day physical theory and at the same time a fascinating analysis of the mind/body problem. He carefully distinguishes between the ideas of determinism, predictability and computability in physical theory. One of his conclusions is 'The present picture of physical reality, particularly in relation to the nature of time, is due for a shake-up.' Note the total absence of the hubris which characterises the biologists. It is as if the biologists didn't know they didn't know. Penrose believes that 'Consciousness is associated with seeing necessary truths', and 'The hallmark of consciousness is a non-algorithmic forming of judgements.' We are clearly in for some interesting surprises in this area. Not all physicists will follow Penrose's controversial view that mind is non-algorithmic, but he refreshingly admits the state of uncertainty in our understanding of the problem.

Summary

In this chapter I have tried to make three points. First, recent advances in molecular biology are producing a powerful biotechnology which will bring benefits, but also social, legal and ethical problems. Second, despite this dramatic advance in our understanding of biology, we are still a long way from a full understanding of life and it is premature to insist that there are irresistable philosophical or theological conclusions to be drawn at this stage. Third, to suggest that recent advances in our understanding of life rules out belief in God is only valid against a very simplistic, though once popular concept of a 'God of the gaps'. The major religions, Christianity in particular, have held a more serious concept of God as Creator, Sustainer and Upholder of all that there is. This is not a recent idea but is biblical and found throughout historic Christianity. The biologists, in coping with their subject, can work with a rather ball-and-spoke model even of biological macromolecules and hence a fairly mechanistic view of life. Physicists find themselves forced to deal with concepts which are less mechanistic and much more analogous to those of theism.

It is certainly not a scientific matter to decide whether or not there is a God, whether or not there is a fundamental explanation of everything in the personal will and purpose of a Creator. It is a decision of a type which is usually called metaphysical. But this does not diminish the importance of the decision. We all, atheists, agnostics and theists alike, make metaphysical decisions, consciously or unconsciously, which involve what we regard as reasonable presuppositions or value judgements; they are unavoidable and we live by our metaphysical decisions. Most of us believe that torture is wrong, that there is truth to be discovered about the natural world, that there is an external world independent of our subjective awareness, that other people have subjective awareness just like our own, and so on. However, justification of these beliefs is not easy. Powerful arguments have been deployed by philosophers purporting to show that justification of these beliefs is not possible. However, these beliefs are not at all arbitrary, but are based not only on empirical evidence, but also considerations of coherence, fruitfulness, comprehensiveness, adequacy and intelligibility as well. On the basis of these criteria and in the light of contemporary biology, belief in God is reasonable.

8

How can I know God, or rather be known by God?

Duncan Vere – Physician

*Professor Duncan W. Vere, MB, BS, MD, FRCP, FFPM.
Born 1929. Educated Friar's School, Bangor, Buckhurst
Hill County High School, and the London Hospital Medical
College (University of London).*
Consultant Physician to the London Hospital since 1968.
*Professor Emeritus of Therapeutics in the University of
London.*
Member, Nuffield Committee on the Profession of Pharmacy.
Member, UK Medicines Commission, 1990.

Imagine, if you will, how you might bring the truth of God
to a boy of six or seven years; then consider such a boy, ill
in bed with bronchitis, whose mother gave him a little
grubby paperback copy of the Book of Revelation in the
Authorised Version to read, because 'it would do you
good'. I did read it, and its first few chapters spoke to my
heart unforgettably; it was true, unpalatably true, in what it
said to me about myself. It was also terrifyingly real in its
imagery about the effects of evil and its judgement; but at
the same time there was the amazing humility and power of
a true and loving Lord who stood outside my heart, not
forcing his way in, but knocking, calling with a warmth and
care that were unmistakably real. The cross was his power

and authority for this; he had given himself for me as for others. My parents later took me to see the reproduction of Holman Hunt's picture in St Paul's Cathedral, London of Jesus knocking at the door. The word and the illustration were both stamped indelibly upon my heart.

Saturday afternoons were times for museum visits and the evenings for Bible studies at Bloomsbury; Harold St John, J.B. Watson and others gave understanding still remembered. Years of wandering, misunderstanding and rebellion followed, with some episodes of faith. I was responsible for dismantling our family Bible readings when I was fourteen; Mother felt it was time for me to try Crusaders, and what a help that class was. I became aware of the courageous witness of its leaders in the war, of charitable help in the East End, and of missionary enterprise abroad. But full grasp and commitment did not come until I was a medical student; the clear evidence of the life of Christ in some fellow students, in Crusader leaders, and at a Billy Graham Crusade were all important elements in convicting a very wayward and devious heart. Even so, I am still greatly troubled by the thought of those I must have stumbled by clumsy and evil strivings at that time.

From then on it has been a story of often painful lessons in learning to live by faith. I could see from some who had achieved greatness in my own family that fame and riches brought no necessary happiness, but often an umbra of deeply wounded souls around the achiever. I can remember a few occasions when God seemed to answer prayer directly. Love for Vera had come literally at first sight, but concern that God's will be done led to silence about it for fourteen prayerful years. She had considered very seriously a call to mission in China; I had considered carefully the test of willingness, but was not called. Suddenly, one memorable day, the answer seemed to become 'yes', and I wrote to her about it. She has been my constant companion, and in every sense we have been members one of the other ever since, and I can never cease to thank God for his answer to our need for one another. Her stroke, some twenty-three years later, seemed for several days likely to prove fatal, or hopelessly disabling. But Psalm 42:11 was sent three times: in the *Daily Light* reading on that very day, in the sermon the following Sunday, and by a minister nearby on his card of condolence. It was a promise that the psalmist, then afflicted, would one day again praise God in his congregation. Every time I hear Vera singing in church now I just thank the Lord; many have not been privileged to receive either such medical skill from colleagues, or such a direct answer to heartfelt prayers by so many members of God's family. Why have we been spared?

Problems: intellectual and moral

There have been problems of many kinds, but it is only in recent years that I have seen their common ground. They began, not surprisingly for a student of applied biology, with the creation-evolution controversy. The evidence from fossils that life of old was not, and could not have been as it is today, was overwhelming and convincing; even my amateur fossil collecting made this clear. It was upsetting to hear people decrying Darwin's work; he was such a painstaking and comprehensive field naturalist and so unwilling to accept assertions which nature counters. Equally, it became clear that much orthodox Christian ideology on such matters came from a frankly superficial grasp of the Genesis story. It is not just about creation; it is largely about God's making creatures from things already made, as the precise use of Hebrew readily discloses. But God is seen as not only the ultimate Creator and Reformer of his universe, but as its continuous Upholder and Provider; these themes recur throughout the Bible. And the precision of the Hebrew over 'creation' contrasts with the lack of biological precision in many other parts of the text, where a spurious precision has been forced upon it by readers of the

English translations. Above all, it is primitive poetry; not biology, not history, not myth, but an observer-told account from a primitive culture of what he had been shown of the works of God, offered to his understanding.

I felt deeply concerned about other young folk who were made to stumble, whether by teachers concerned to attack Scripture, or by those seeking to defend it. I felt led to make a soundstrip about the problem, a technically weak production which none the less circulated for some time around schools. My experiences in preparing this were startling, and still hard to understand; being a young and then impecunious doctor I lacked the funds for the job. But there was no mistaking the call to do it. A patient gave front-aluminised mirrors for a single lens reflex camera. The lens was sold to me very cheaply; the government surplus stockist did not know what it was, and though I took it back to him to tell him that he had undercharged, he refused unwisely to accept! I can remember praying one morning for materials to illustrate the argument; as I left the house there was a dead melanic peppered moth on the doormat. Belemnites were needed, and turned up in an ornamental stone wall in our local garden nursery. Graptolites (*Tetragraptus*) were found when I stepped out of a coach on a five-minute journey break, an unusual experience for any fossil hunter, and so it went on and on. I still don't know why I was to do that work; one day it may be known. I do know that I had become a convinced 'theistic evolutionist', who accepts creation but not in the constricted sense forced upon that doctrine by many of its sincere, and perhaps misunderstanding proponents. More recent scientific discoveries, such as the continual and intermittent synthesis of elements of increasing atomic number in stars by the 'regular' and 'swift' pathways, have greatly increased our understanding of God's creative and upholding powers.

The next problem was resurrection; how can it be conceived of in terms of space and time? The startlingly obvious answer is, of course, that it cannot because it is from eternity; but more of that shortly. It, too, brought surprises. It had become clear to me, from reading Paul's first letter to the Christians at Corinth, that the resurrection body promised by Christ would resemble his own, be that of an identifiable individual, but of different material from this 'body of humiliation'. Having published something to this effect, I received several protests, including one from a well known and loved evangelical leader, insisting that the body which will be raised is this present flesh. Unfortunately, Paul was not around to be consulted, but I hope he would not have thought that I had misquoted him. It seemed clear at least that if God has called my mind, or anyone's mind, into being in the first place, it will not be a problem for him to reconstruct it in other materials; the real problems are our space-time boundaries, our hidden and implicit argument that because we know one version of space-time there can be no others. And there is our unbelief in God; I cannot see any other problems about resurrection. The important things seem to be to recognise that God has done it once, but that those whom Jesus restored to life during his ministry were different; they were restored to *this* life, not resurrected.

The next problem was the Bible's teachings about God's sovereign choice of those who are his children, and their exercise of freewill. This was made much easier by the recognition that the Bible clearly exposes these doctrines in a context of complementarity; there are many examples of this, and I can remember marking them in my Bible as a student (eg, Phil 1:29). The problem is again one of space-time versus eternity. I make my choice in space-time—God chooses me from eternity. The fact that the Bible states such paradoxes unequivocally and repeatedly came to me to be evidence for its 'God-breathed' status, not the reverse; if God is to be God, he must transcend me as well as indwell me. A God who could be 'caught under a jar', as it were, in space-time, could never be a significant God, the God of the Bible.

I also spent much time concerned with the apparent design in nature, the kind of doubts and discernings stirred so eloquently but atheistically by Richard Dawkins in *The Blind Watchmaker*. But it has always seemed clear to me that just because one cannot use Paley's logic to prove the existence of a Designer, and just because one may show that in some restricted areas structures can arise through apparent random forces acting upon matter, neither evidence necessarily disproves design. Nor should the design argument ever be pursued in isolation, in an information vacuum. For once the Designer speaks his nature, and reveals his plans, the quality of the evidence of revelation-taken-with-nature becomes totally different from that of unaided observation alone. It coheres in a different, and utterly meaningful way. Again, we are returned to space-time as our source of evidence alone, or eternity *with* space-time if God speaks into our partial understandings from his realm beyond space-time.

Then there are moral problems in abundance in the practice of medicine. Chief among these is the tension between 'paternalism' and 'autonomy'; within my own medical lifetime of only forty years the emphasis has shifted right across from the 'doctor knowing best' to the 'patient's informed wish being foremost' in our society. With this has come an implicit rejection of almost all moral principles drawn from without an individual ('deontology'), and the ascendance of many moral absurdities as 'received truths'. To give one example, there is the concept of an 'unwanted child', which is usually held to justify 'termination of pregnancy'. But how can there exist a state of essential unwantedness (it is the potential mother's state, not the child's, which determines the choice), and in what other circumstances of life can the wish of one determine legitimately the life-fate of another? More seriously, whose autonomy is being regarded? Many other problems create tensions, not least that between home, wife and family on one hand, care of patients, teaching and research on another, and the local church. It is difficult to render to Caesar and to God what belongs to each when their timetables and need pressures conflict and do not coincide! But through prayer and thoughtful study the Lord can show a way through, given willingness to hear him. Many of this world's pressures have no necessary force, and are based on perceptions which exclude God from consideration, whether by habitual frame of reference or from deliberate choice.

Who or what has particularly helped me? Like any other person who has come to faith, I have been surrounded by those who believe that God cannot be known, by those who think that one can never be sure, and by those who believe but express their dedication to one form of belief by belabouring other believers whose thoughts are incongruent with their rigidities. The helps have come through seeing Christ unmistakably in the lives of other Christians, and by working through the problems aided by splendidly gifted mentors. I cannot single out any who are still alive, but the Bible teaching of Harold St John, Alan Stibbs and Martyn Lloyd-Jones, and the sanctified logic of Donald MacKay stand out among those who have passed on. One is deeply grateful to them all.

God in the world

Those puzzles about miracles, resurrection, freewill and predestination, creation and evolution have all seemed to move towards a common solution, the clues to which were first brought to my awareness by things that Donald MacKay wrote or said. He spoke of 'cosmic events' (the Fall, the crucifixion, resurrection). He spoke of our current awareness as being like a television image or the standing wave pattern beneath a waterfall; a dynamic reality which could be switched off, or dissolved at source, and which depended on its source moment by moment (see p 204f). Oddly, these pictures helped only in part, and it was not until I had worked through a book about differential geometry (for medical research connected with drug receptor theory) that understanding came. If there is a God, the sort of transcendent, yet indwelling God that the Bible so insistently portrays, then he must 'inhabit eternity' and so exist in a space which is 'unknowable' as such. Suppose that we call the dimensions of that space R_n, where n is an enormous number. We, by contrast, are presently shut in to space-time (R_3+t), Einstein's four-dimensional manifold. Modern (Riemannian) geometry shows how spaces in R_n and (R_3+t) must needfully interrelate; R_n can be 'mapped' upon R_3+t, with precise rules about the meanings which can or cannot be inferred about such a 'mapping'. These rules suggest many things about possible, or 'legitimate' relationships between God and man, such as

1 It is not possible to assert from observation of (R_3+t) that R_n cannot exist.

2 It is not possible to argue that R_n cannot be 'mapped onto' (R_3+t) (cf, 'incarnation', 'indwelling'). It can be so, but only by reduction or loss of information.

3 It is not possible to create out of (R_3+t) a satisfactory 'map' ('image') of R_n; to attempt to do so is approaching idolatry.

4 Whereas these ideas cannot show *how* R_n interacts with (R_3+t), they can show how they *could* do so.

5 Individuals organised in R_n cannot communicate unambiguously with those in (R_3+t) (compare aircraft flying in (R_3+t), mapped upon a radar screen in (R_2+t), and seeming to 'crash').

6 However, individuals in R_n can communicate with those in (R_3+t) if they reveal themselves in '(R_3+t) language'. (Donald MacKay wrote much about the strict and necessary rules for affirming 'complementarity' in such exchanges.) For reasons 1 to 6, the evidence for Christ's claims must be received by faith in a degree, and cannot in their nature be discerned solely by human

sight. But this is not a leap in the dark; it stands as evidence.

7 Further, when seeking confirmation of ideas from R_n, this cannot be affirmed rigidly or formally from material projected in (R_3+t), whether that material is an event or a set of Bible texts or whatever. For example, one of my most painful experiences in medicine came when a lovely young woman died from a rare carotid artery dissection; her father and husband came to the ward together and in their mutual tragedy one man saw God's inscrutable mercy and the other the evidence that he did not exist. What could I say; both were highly intelligent, but I believe that neither had *logic* with them at that most dreadful moment in their lives; one had positive, the other negative beliefs.

Fear God: that is the whole duty of man

In short, I now have a model for understanding the common thread in each of those diverse paradoxes which have plagued Jewish and Christian apologists throughout time: all have a common stem, the problems of a transcendent, yet indwelling God and finite people cast within time in intercommunion. But I can also see that one of the strongest evidences that Scripture is God's 'breathed' revelation to mankind lies in the fact that it refers repeatedly and uncompromisingly to things which cannot be understood in (R_3+t) alone, but which become filled with meaning as 'mappings' from R_n upon space-time. The model which helped me most to grasp this was the sight of Loweswater in the Lake District, stirred to a lovely pattern by an offshore breeze. The water and the air exist in invisible motions in (R_3+t). But the surface, in (R_2+t), revealed their interaction visibly in amazing beauty. Is our 'real' universe, in (R_3+t), just a 'hypersurface' among greater but invisible realities in R_n? Why cannot a resurrection body not be a 'map' of the 'real' me, taken out of (R_3+t) upon R_s (where $S > 3$)? If 'evolution' is what the 'creation' looks like mapped on to (R_3+t), why can't it look like creation in the timeless 'world' of R_n, just as in light waves electricity looked at sideways appears as magnetism? And if I choose to trust God in (R_3+t), why can't he choose me 'from before the foundation of the world' in a Christ 'slain' in R_n? Did not Jesus himself tell us that the movement of the Spirit is like the wind; we *cannot* see where it comes or whence it goes, but we *do* observe the evidence of its efects in (R_3+t)—we 'hear the sound of it' (Jn 3:8). The essential problems are our tunnel vision, our unwillingness to receive anything as true which we cannot understand, our insistence upon making the measure of an infinite God our finite grasp of him; this is the staggering arrogance of which I had been guilty! Scientific understanding is a splendid thing, a gift of God. But I had to come to see that though it can describe much, it can account for, and can regulate nothing. Least of all can it account for origins or destinies. My great regret is that this took my very limited understanding so long to grasp.

And what of the moral problems in medicine? Having sieved twice through Scripture to collect an inventory of ethical passages, I can now see how important moral principle, or deontology, is. The Bible contains a treasure store of stated principles and of 'worked examples', with a divine commentary. There is a strong autonomy indeed, but guarded by moral principle. There is moral consequence, but this again is guarded in the same way; moral choice is lifted away from the relativism and contradictoriness of so much that passes for ethics today; the moral stance of Scripture is squarely upon the individual worth of persons, as responsible towards God and one another. It is in obedience to his revealed will, freely given by individuals,

and not always as even the church has perceived it historically, that moral liberty is found. So it is that I believe Jesus
saves us in the past, in the present, and will save us yet
beyond this passing time.

9

Can Science and Christianity Both Be True?

Colin Humphreys – Materials scientist

Professor Colin J.Humphreys, MA, BSc, PhD, FIM, F Inst Phys.
Born 1941. Educated Luton Grammar School and Imperial College, London.
Goldsmiths' Professor of Materials Science, University of Cambridge since 1992.
Professor of Materials Science in the University of Cambridge 1990–92.
Previously Professor of Materials Engineering, Liverpool University, 1985–89.
Member, Science and Engineering Research Council since 1988.
Chairman, Materials Science and Engineering Commission, SERC since 1988.

Dorothy Sayers is famous for her detective stories featuring Lord Peter Wimsey. She was also a Christian and in one of her books *The Dogma is the Drama* she records the following interview with a typical man in the street:

Question: What is Christian faith?
Answer (by man in the street): Resolutely shutting your eyes to scientific fact.

In similar vein, Sir Richard Gregory, a former editor of *Nature*, wrote:

My grandfather preached the gospel of Christ
My father preached the gospel of Socialism
I preach the gospel of Science.

These quotations illustrate the popular belief that science and Christianity cannot both be true. In my life the question 'Is Christianity true?' has cropped up in various ways and I will write about some of these in this Chapter. It was as a science student at university that I first wrestled with this question. Problems I have faced since then have included whether biblical miracles were real historical events and whether the theory of evolution can be true. I will write briefly about these topics in this Chapter, ending with a particular personal interest: the use of astronomy to establish the date of various biblical events.

Is Christianity true? A personal conclusion

I had come to London to study physics at Imperial College and my accommodation in the first year of my undergraduate life was like a scene from a play. I lived in a house in Chiswick: the landlady was French, she had lived in England for forty years yet she only spoke six words of English. Her husband was Greek and he was a chef at a famous London club. Also in the house were two other students: Paul, a first year pharmacist, and Michael, a medical student who had lived for several years in the house. Both the French landlady and her Greek husband were superb cooks, and we must have been the best fed students in London. However there was an unusual condition about living in the house—the landlady would only accept students who spoke French! I scraped by.

'By chance', Paul and Michael were both Christians. Paul had been brought up in a small denomination known as Strict Baptists. At university he rebelled somewhat against his strict upbringing, gave a mean imitation of Elvis Presley on the guitar, became highly extrovert and is the only person I have known literally to go out with a different girl every night of a particular week. Michael, on the other hand, was quiet and studious (and an Anglican). I had been brought up by Christian parents, went to church and Sunday school, and became a Christian at about age eleven. At school I believed that evolution was nonsense and gave my biology teacher a hard time! However the year before I went to university I started having serious doubts about the existence of God and I rejected Christianity (without telling anybody).

I resolved to work the matter out in my first year at London. For me the key question was 'Is Christianity true?' I decided to read through one gospel, a little each night, and also one book about becoming a Christian. I started in a very sceptical frame of mind. I tried to imagine being there in first century Palestine as Jesus spoke, and to think if the words made sense. I had never realised before how outrageous were many of the claims of Jesus. It seemed to me that there were only three possibilities: either Jesus was who he claimed to be, or he was mad, or it was all a cruel hoax. Similarly with the Resurrection: either it was true or else it was a cruel hoax. Which was correct?

I agonised over this for some weeks, and I did not find the answer obvious. I discussed the matter with no one. I felt it had to be between me and God, if there was a God. Finally I became convinced that Christianity was true, but, and this I found really surprising, I didn't want it. I rejected Christianity knowing it to be true. I knew this was intellectually dishonest but I did not want to make the commitment. Having reached the stage of rejecting Christianity I planned to stop going to church. However Paul and Michael went, so I went along with them. In any case, there were some attractive girls at the church! I became a secret non-Christian.

After the Sunday night service the minister would have a group of us back to his house for coffee, biscuits and a chat.

After leaving the minister's house on one particular night I found myself walking along the street with someone who worked locally whom I did not know at all well. As we were walking along the street he suddenly said he would like to be a Christian and he asked me how. The others in the group were further up the road and well ahead of us. My brain raced as I considered the honest course of action. I was well able to tell him how to become a Christian, but would it be intellectually honest to tell him something I had chosen not to believe myself? On the other hand I could tell him that I was not a believer, but would it be right for me to say something which might destroy his search for Christian belief? After a few moments thought I said he should go and speak with the minister of the church. I then went back to my lodgings knowing that I should no longer resist what I knew to be true and that night I committed myself afresh to Christ. I was delighted that the other man did visit the minister and he too became a Christian.

A few months after my decision I started doubting again. Once more I went through the arguments whether or not Christianity was true, and again I decided it was. Doubts returned periodically, but slowly diminished. There were times when being a Christian was like walking on a tight rope. For me the key question each time was 'Is it true?' I have not had these doubts for a number of years, but I have always had great sympathy for the disciple known as Doubting Thomas!

Scientific truth and Christian truth

So far I have been writing about the truth of Christianity. But how does this relate to scientific truth? There is a widespread belief that science and Christianity occupy different territories. Thus it is often held that science is concerned with the material world and Christianity with the spiritual world. A basic problem with any territorial model is that battles at the boundaries are probably inevitable. A famous general once said that one-country maps were useless because most battles were fought at the boundaries between two countries. I am unhappy with a territorial model for science because although the limits of science can probably be defined today, they will have changed dramatically in 100 years' time. In principle I believe any topic should be open for scientific study. Similarly I am unhappy with a territorial model for Christianity, since the God revealed to us in the Bible and through Christ is the God of all, both spiritual and material. Paul writes, 'For by him [Christ] all things were created, things in heaven and on earth, visible and invisible . . . all things were created by him and for him (Colossians 1:16). Thus I believe that science and Christianity are concerned with the same territory: the universe and all that it contains—nothing is barred.

The building of truth

I have found it very helpful to think of truth in terms of a set of architect's drawings of a building. A complex building will have side views (elevations), views from the top (plans), and sections drawn at different levels. There will be common elements where two drawings meet. Each drawing (eg, an elevation) is complete in itself. All drawings should fit together, although it is often very difficult for the untrained eye to see this.

The analogy with truth is obvious. Truth is a unity—there is one building of truth. However more than one drawing is necessary for a full description. Each drawing is different because it is from a different viewpoint. Thus I believe that science and Christianity describe the same territory, the same building of truth, but from different viewpoints. The master architect has ensured that all the viewpoints fit together, but to the untrained eye that is often not easy to see.

It is dangerous to pursue analogies too far, but we can take the building of truth model a little further. We don't even have the individual drawings! It is as if each drawing is broken up into a jigsaw puzzle. Scientists are trying to reconstruct the jigsaw of scientific truth. We may feel that many of the pieces are now in position, but I suspect that we have only just started (the quantity of our scientific knowledge about the universe is much less than the quantity of our ignorance). Similarly with Christianity. Some pieces of the jigsaw are in the Old Testament, some key pieces were revealed to us by Jesus, further pieces were revealed to the New Testament writers but still 'we see through a glass darkly', as we try to reconstruct the Christian view of the universe, including mankind.

In attempting to understand architects' drawings it is useful to focus on common boundaries, eg, where a side elevation and an end elevation meet. Similarly in science and Christianity, common boundaries (of two incomplete jigsaws) are particularly important places which should be seen not as areas of conflict but as places where our understanding of truth may be advanced, and a few more pieces put in the jigsaw. For example, was creation in six literal days? It is my belief that if the early chapters of Genesis are read without preconceptions (very difficult!) then it is not possible to be sure whether the author intended them to be literal or not. On the one hand the creation account has a rather matter-of-fact style, but on the other hand pictorial language is used. For example the account describes 'the tree of life', which few people take as a literal tree when it is later referred to in the last book of the Bible, the book of Revelation. However, science also reveals to us information about the creation of the world. Because the building of truth is a unity, the scientific viewpoint of creation can help to reconstruct the part of the Christian jigsaw of truth dealing with creation. We will return later to the creation/evolution issue. At this point let me emphasise a key general point: the God revealed to us through Jesus is the same God who is revealed to us through the scientific study of the universe he created. If conflicts arise it is therefore because either our understanding of Christianity, or of science, or of both, is incorrect (ie we have misplaced some of the jigsaw pieces). I believe there can be no conflict if our understanding of science and Christianity are both correct.

What is distinctive about the scientific viewpoint of truth? The aim of science is to describe and understand the universe (including man) in terms of mechanisms, theories and laws. As a materials scientist I try to explain the macroscopic properties of materials (strength, electrical and thermal conductivity, etc) in terms of the position and movement of atoms, ions and electrons. Scientists also use their understanding of mechanisms, theories and laws to predict the future. Scientists essentially ask the question 'how?', and try to answer this question in terms of mechanisms. Thus the jigsaw of the scientific viewpoint of truth is built up.

What is distinctive about the Christian viewpoint of truth? Whereas scientists mainly ask the question 'how?', eg, 'how did we get here?', Christians mainly ask the question 'why?', eg, 'why are we here?' However, Christians also sometimes ask the question 'how?' and scientists also sometimes ask the question 'why?'—there are common boundaries on the building of truth. Scientific truth is mainly objective (eg, the pen I am writing this with has a certain mass which can be measured and agreed upon by scientists throughout the world). Christian truth is both objective and subjective, and the subjective part is important. Many aspects of reality can be known only by personal involvement, for example the love of one person for another. The Christian truth that God committed himself to us through Jesus can only be known if we commit ourselves to him. The building of truth is therefore complex and contains both objective and subjective truth.

There is another most important way in which the

building of truth is complex—it contains different floors and levels. We first learn science in a simplified way. For example we are taught at school that Ohm's Law, $V = IR$, is a universal law. Whereas it is true that $V = IR$ holds in the everyday world, for extremely thin wires Ohm's Law breaks down. However we don't teach school pupils about this exception; if we attempted to teach school pupils all the complexities of science they would never learn anything! We start with simple truths and work up to more complex truths. So it is with Christianity. Paul writes of feeding new Christians on milk, like babies, but also that we should progress to a diet of meatier truths. Some scientific truths are unchanged however much we learn: for example, the value of the speed of light seems to be a constant truth. Similarly some Christian truths are unchanged on whatever level of the building of truth we consider them: for example, I believe the Resurrection to be an event in history which is both a milk-truth and a meat-truth.

Miracles

Can a scientist believe in miracles such as the Resurrection? To understand miracles we must first understand 'normal' events. For scientists, normal events are described by theories and laws. Laws are well established theories which have survived many tests. Laws therefore describe the past: they do not prescribe the future (ie, predict what must happen in the future) but they do raise our expectations to a very high degree. For example, we would be astonished if a predicted solar eclipse did not occur.

What is the Christian view of normal events? A few years ago one of the Christmas cards I received had on the front a picture of a chef holding in his outstretched hands a giant spherical Christmas pudding. Underneath the sender had written his own caption, the first line of a famous Negro spiritual 'He holds the whole world in his hands'. It was a brilliant analogy. The chef was outside of, and distinct from, his pudding, yet the creative genius of the chef was within each morsel. The chef was upholding the pudding. He could be said to have created the pudding in a few hours, yet the ingredients had taken much longer to develop.

The analogy of course is obvious. God is both the creator and the upholder of the universe. Paul writing to the Colossians says 'All things were created by him [Christ] and for him. He is before all things and in him all things hold together' (Colossians 1:16, 17). When Paul spoke to a non-Christian audience in Athens he said, 'He gives life and breath and all things to all men. In him we live and move and exist' (Acts 17:28). The message is clear: Christ continually sustains and upholds the universe, including mankind.

Some years ago Jonathan Miller presented a television series called 'The Body in Question'. In one programme the television cameras filmed statues of famous men and a fountain in the garden of a stately home, and Jonathan Miller asked the question, 'What is the human body more like; is it like one of these statues or is it like the fountain?' The obvious answer was that our body is more like a statue, but the cameras zoomed in to show them crumbling away, whereas the fountain was being constantly renewed. Jonathan Miller said the human body was more like the fountain: our body cells, skin, nails, etc, are constantly being renewed (of course the analogy cannot be extended to old age).

The biblical picture of God is not of a being who created the universe like a statue (with a clockwork mechanism) and then left it to decay, like an absentee landlord. Instead God is depicted as constantly upholding the universe, both externally like the chef holding up the pudding, and also acting within the very fabric of the universe. The analogy I like best of God's upholding is that of the singer and the song. The song depends totally on being uttered by the singer, moment by moment. So it is, I believe, with God and the universe, including mankind. We owe our moment-by-moment existence to the upholding of God.

The consistency of God

Ringing through the pages of the Bible is the message that God is consistent and not capricious. For example, 'summer and winter, seedtime and harvest shall not fail' (Genesis 8:22), or 'Jesus Christ, the same yesterday, today and forever' (Hebrews 13:8).

Scientists who are Christians believe that because God is consistent, therefore the universe is consistent, and hence it can be described by theories and laws. There are some eminent science historians who argue that the reason science flourished in Europe in the seventeenth century, and not previously in ancient China, Egypt, India, Babylon or Greece, brilliant observers that they were of natural phenomena, was because many of the early European scientists (Newton, Kepler, etc) were Christians who believed in a consistent God and an orderly universe. Thus Newton realised that the force of gravity on earth that attracted the anecdotal apple to the ground was the same force of gravity that acted throughout the universe and was responsible for the planets moving around the sun. Kepler said, 'scientists try to think God's thoughts after him', and he looked for elegant mathematical models of planetary motion. These early scientists were driven by the belief that God and his creation were consistent and not capricious.

However, this raises a major problem concerning miracles. If at least some miracles are real events, how can this be reconciled with not only our scientific belief in an orderly universe but also with our Christian belief in a God who is consistent and not capricious? It is helpful to consider some specific miracles to see how this problem can be resolved.

Crossing the Jordan

Joshua 3:15 records, 'As soon as the priests reached the Jordan the water from upstream stopped flowing. It piled up in a heap a great distance away at a town called Adam, while the water flowing down to the Dead Sea was completely cut off'. Joshua then records that about 40,000 Israelites crossed over.

The Bible consists of various types of writing: history, poetry, parables etc. When considering miracles we must seriously ask the question whether the author intended his account to be understood as history or not. This is not always easy to decide; however it seems to me that the above description in Joshua is meant to be understood as an historical event.

As a Christian I believe that God is all-powerful and can do anything. However I also believe that he will not do anything that is against his character. Since God is a consistent God I believe it is right always to look for a consistent, not a capricious, explanation of miracles. I therefore believe that we should always look first for an understanding of miracles in terms of scientific mechanisms, although I realise that not all miracles can be explained in this way (see later), at least not with our current scientific understanding.

Returning to the 'crossing the Jordan' miracle, in 1979 Amos Nur, a geophysicist at Stanford University, studied in detail historical earthquakes on the Jericho fault. He found that in 1927 there was an earthquake which caused mud slides along the River Jordan at a place called Damia, about 40km north of Jericho. These mud slides temporarily cut-off the flow of the river Jordan. Nur then found that Damia used to be called Adam, the place described in Joshua as being where the river Jordan was stopped, and he also found records of other occasions when an earthquake had caused mud slides that had stopped the river Jordan in this way. He states, 'Adam is now Damia, the site of the

1927 mud slides which cut off the flow of the Jordan. Such cut offs, typically lasting one to two days, have also been recorded in 1906, 1834, 1546, 1534, 1267 and 1160'. Nur adds that the description of the stoppage of the Jordan in Joshua 3:15 is so typical of earthquakes in this region that little doubt can be left of the reality of this event in Joshua's time.

God is all-powerful and therefore stopping the flow of the Jordan could have been a special supernatural intervention of God. However the key question to ask is not 'what could God do?' but 'what did God do?' Was stopping the Jordan a special intervention of God or was it due to a natural mechanism? We have seen that there is clear historical evidence of the Jordan being stopped by earthquake-produced mud slides many times in the past at precisely the place, Adam, specified in the book of Joshua. There is strong evidence therefore that an earthquake was the natural mechanism which stopped the Jordan in the time of Joshua. Does this mechanistic explanation mean that the event was not a miracle? No: it was still a miracle, but a miracle of timing. At precisely the time when Joshua and 40,000 Israelites needed to cross the Jordan an earthquake occurred causing mud-slides which blocked the river's flow. God upholds the universe with perfect timing. Many 'miracles' happen today through natural mechanisms. For example, materials scientists provide artificial hips that enable the lame to walk, surgeons perform cataract operations that enable the blind to see. Just because we can understand scientifically these modern healing methods does not make them any less the hand of God.

The burning bush

'Moses saw that although the bush was on fire it did not burn up' (Exodus 3:2).

At first sight this description seems very curious.

However there are bush species, for example *Dictamnus albus,* the flowers of which emit a volatile gas which can catch fire spontaneously if certain conditions are met simultaneously: intense sunlight, high temperature, large bush, many flowers open, no wind and no flying insects to disperse the gas. If all the above conditions coincide the gas around the bush can have a sufficient concentration and be at a sufficient temperature that its flash-point is reached. The gas then catches fire spontaneously and burns although the bush itself does not burn (somewhat similarly gas burns above a gas ring without the ring itself burning). This effect can be produced in a greenhouse, but a bush catching fire spontaneously is very rare in nature (it has been reported in Central Europe, near Warsaw, in 1965). It is rare in nature because of all the conditions that must be satisfied simultaneously.

Was the bush that Moses saw newly created by God for the occasion, or was it an existing bush the flowers of which emitted a volatile gas? Again the key question to ask is not 'what could God do?' but 'what did God do?', given that God is consistent and not capricious. To me the answer is clear. This was an existing normal bush. However, at this particular time when Moses passed by the conditions were right for spontaneous combustion: many flowers emitting a volatile gas were open, there was no wind nor flying insects, etc. But the biggest miracle of timing was that when this spontaneous burning occurred, Moses was there, God spoke to him, Moses responded, he led God's people out of Egypt and this (in popular language) changed the course of history.

The Resurrection

Are all miracles 'miracles of timing' explicable in terms of natural mechanisms? I believe that many are, but others, for example the healing miracles performed by Jesus and his Resurrection, we cannot explain by natural mechanisms (at least not with our present scientific knowledge). In these cases God appears to be operating differently from usual, but how can this be if God is consistent and not capricious?

Imagine standing behind a pianist as he plays the piano from memory. If his fingers normally land on the white keys, but every time he goes to play an F he plays the black F sharp instead you can deduce the key signature (G major) of the composition. The key signature is at the start of the musical score and it is the rule given by the composer for playing his music. God, the Master Composer of the universe, has established its key signature. We do not have the score of the universe, but by careful observation scientists can establish the rules by which it operates: we call these rules the laws of nature (of course we may be wrong about some of these).

A musical composer is not bound by his own rules. He is free to decide that at a particular place in the music he wants an additional sharp or flat; these local deviations from the key signature rules are called accidentals. With a great composer these accidentals are never capricious, they are always carefully placed and consistent with what the composer wants to achieve. They make sweeter music. (Try playing a Beethoven sonata as written and then without the accidentals.) Similarly God is not bound by the rules he has established for the universe. He is free to uphold it moment by moment in any way he chooses. However he is a consistent God, and therefore any 'local accidental', any change in his method of upholding, must be consistent with what he wants to achieve. It cannot be capricious, it must make sweeter music, it must be consistent with the overall purpose of God.

Jesus, the son of God, had perfect love. It made more sense, not less sense, for him to heal the sick. It was totally consistent with his character. In Peter's first sermon, at Pentecost, he states that God raised Jesus from the dead 'because it was impossible for death to keep its hold on him' (Acts 2:24). Peter saw the Resurrection as being inevitable, not incredible. If Jesus really was the Son of God then death could not hold him. The Resurrection fully accords with God being consistent not capricious, and was planned by God before the creation of the universe.

Many people think of miracles as interventions of God, and people often pray for God to intervene in the world. While this may be a convenient way to think from our point of view, the notion of God intervening is inconsistent with the biblical picture of God upholding the universe moment by moment. God is not a passive God who sometimes intervenes: God is always active. On rare occasions he chooses to act differently from usual. On less rare occasions events occur which to us seem to be astonishing co-incidences of timing. Both these types of events we usually refer to as miracles. Both are equally the hand of God.

Creation and evolution

I was brought up to believe that animals and plants did not develop over millions of years by a process of evolution, but that each species was directly created by God. This belief is called creationism and it is shared by a great many people. When I went to university I started to question the beliefs I had held, and later I wrote a booklet on creation and evolution, aimed at secondary school pupils (the booklet has recently been translated into Chinese). The key question to be asked is 'Is evolution or creationism true?'

An enormous amount has been written about evolution. One of the critical questions is how old is life on earth? According to the theory of evolution it is many millions of years old, whereas many creationists believe life to have originated only about 6,000 years ago. This is clearly a question that science should be able to resolve.

It is well known that the ages of trees can be determined

by counting the rings in the trunk. This method of dating is called dendrochronology. Some trees live for an astonishingly long time. The oldest known living object, plant or animal, in the world is a tree: living bristlecone pine trees exist which are 4,900 years old. A tree's rings can vary a great deal in colour and thickness from year to year, depending on the local climate. By counting tree-rings from both living and dead trees, and matching characteristic patterns in them, a continuous tree-ring dating sequence has been built up, extending back for 8,200 years. The importance of this dating method is that it is accurate and absolute.

If it is assumed that the early chapters of Genesis are literally true, and that the genealogies given in the Bible have no missing generations, then it is possible to reconstruct the human family tree, with Adam and Eve at the top. Bishop Ussher was the first to calculate from the genealogies the date when Adam should have been created: 4004BC. Therefore if the early chapters of Genesis are interpreted literally the world was created in 4004BC.

However, we know beyond reasonable doubt that trees existed on the earth 8,200 years ago. Thus either early Genesis should not be interpreted literally or the genealogies are incomplete (ie, should not be interpreted literally) or both. We can say with reasonable certainty from tree ring dating that those creationists who believe the world was created in 4004BC are wrong.

Other creationists believe that the earth's age is about 10,000 years, that the early chapters of Genesis are literally true, but that the genealogies were not intended to be a totally complete record. To investigate these claims a dating method is needed that goes further back in time than tree-ring dating. Various such methods exist: radiocarbon dating can be used to date animals and plants for the last 70,000 years. For older specimens, particularly rocks, radio-uranium and radio-potassium methods can be used. These methods indicate that the oldest rocks known on earth are about 3,900 millions years old, and that the ages of meteorites found on earth are about 4,600 million years. The earliest evidence for life comes from traces of the outlines of colonies of bacteria in rocks about 3,000 million years old. Sea snail fossils have been found which are about 600 million years old, and the first whales appeared about 50 million years ago.

There is therefore strong evidence that the Earth is very old, and that different types of animals emerged at intervals of many millions of years. However, as we have noted above, many creationists believe the Earth is only 10,000 years old, or even less. How can they believe this in the face of the scientific evidence? First, some creationists claim that radioactive dating methods are unreliable. But even if radioactive dates are wrong by as much as 100%, which is extremely unlikely, the Earth is still many millions of years old. Second, many creationists believe in the theory of Apparent Age, which is a very clever theory, but which strikes at the heart of the belief that God reveals himself to us through his created universe.

The creationist theory of apparent age

In 1857 Philip Henry Gosse published a book entitled *Omphalos: An Attempt to Untie the Geological Knot*. Omphalos is the Greek word for navel. The navel is of course what remains when the umbilical cord is cut from a new-born baby. Did Adam have a navel, even though he was not born? Of course he did, said Gosse. God created him the way he intended all human beings to be. (In a recent 1990 issue of *New Scientist* the cover depicted Adam with a navel, and this was questioned in subsequent correspondence!) In the same way, Gosse argued, the trees God created were fully grown trees with rings in them: thus although the creation took place in 4004BC, Gosse argued that if we try to date it scientifically it appears older.

Modern creationists have updated this idea, so that it is argued that God created rocks in 4004BC having an apparent age of 3,000 million years if dated using scientific methods.

Logically it is impossible to tell the difference between:
(i) a world which really is very old
(ii) a world which is young but has been given a perfect appearance of age.

However, sheer common sense suggests that (i) must be preferred to (ii). Again, the key question is not 'what could God do?', but 'what did God do?' God does not deceive us by leaving old fossils lying about. The God who created all life is the same God as he who reveals his creation to us. This is central to my beliefs as a scientist and as a Christian. Since our study of the world shows clearly that it is very old and that life has emerged over millions of years then this is the timescale over which God has created life on Earth. It follows that the early chapters of Genesis should not be interpreted literally.

For most of the time the universe has existed there has been neither man nor woman. We occupy just a tiny speck of space-time on one out of millions of planets. This makes me feel very humble. On the other hand it has taken an immense journey through time to produce us. God is the Master Mind who planned this great journey: that makes us something special. Just as life on Earth appears to have developed by a process of evolution from single cells, so the Earth itself appears to have evolved from the original Big Bang. It seems that evolution is the general way in which God chooses to work, and it fills me with wonder that the whole of the universe and the whole of life were encapsulated in the very first concentration of matter and energy, rather like a great tree is encapsulated in a tiny seed.

The major way in which Christians and non-Christians differ in their view of the theory of evolution is that for many non-Christians 'pure chance, absolutely free but blind, is at the very root of evolution ... Neither the duty nor the destiny of man have been written down' (the distinguished biologist Jacques Monod). Christians cannot agree with this because they believe that life has a plan and a purpose. The topics of scientific chance and classical chaos are complex and outside the scope of this chapter. Although both may play key roles in evolution, I believe that God is in charge and that evolution is the way he chose to carry out his creation. If life emerged from a primeval soup then God was the Master Chef.

Dating biblical events

Christianity is not some vague set of beliefs: it is based upon real historical events, for example, the crucifixion, and if we can pinpoint in time these events we strengthen the historical basis of the Christian faith. We may also understand certain events better if we know when they occurred, and hence can set them precisely in the social and political climate at the time.

Chronology is the backbone of history, and most history textbooks are written around a framework of the dates on which certain events occurred. On the other hand, dates are strangely absent from most commentaries on both the Old and New Testament books, even though the writers of the Bible were often keen to date events according to their own calendar systems, usually based upon the reigns of kings. For example, Isaiah had an important vision 'in the year that king Uzziah died' (Isaiah 6:1), John the Baptist started his ministry 'in the fifteenth year of the reign of Tiberius Caesar' (Luke 3:1). We need to know the corresponding dates in our BC/AD calendar as a starting point for dating events such as the crucifixion.

One of my young daughters once had a book called *Great Men of History,* which devoted a few pages to each person selected (I hope some women were included also!). In the front of the book was a list of the people featured, with their dates of birth and of death. Definite dates were assigned to each person except one, Jesus Christ, against whom was typed 'born 4BC (?), died 30AD (?)'. This uncertainty must raise doubts in the minds of some people about whether Jesus really existed, and I have made it a particular personal interest to use my very limited spare time to try to pin down more accurately the dates of some important biblical events.

Science, particularly astronomy, has a key role to play in this since ancient writings, including the Bible, sometimes feature astronomical events (eg, eclipses) occurring in a certain year of the reign of a particular king. If we can identify the astronomical event and calculate when it occurred, and if the text is reliable, then we can have certainty and precision in dating the reign of the king. I find this use of astronomy and history applied to dating biblical events complicated and fascinating. It is like unravelling a mystery in a detective story with very limited clues. I would love to do this full time!

My first foray into this arena was to attempt to date the crucifixion, with the help of an astronomer colleague. The date we determined, 3 April AD33, was not a new date, but we produced some new evidence. It is important to realise that Christians will not always agree about matters because the evidence is often incomplete, or because our understanding is incomplete. In the case of dating the crucifixion there is not enough evidence to be 100% certain, but I would claim there is enough to say that there is a very high probability (say 95%) that the date of the crucifixion was on 3 April AD33. The biblical evidence fits this date remarkably well.

I was amazed at the interest shown in our paper (published in *Nature* **306**: 743–746, 1983). I stopped counting after 500 reprint requests and letters were received in the first few weeks after publication. News about this dating of the crucifixion featured in national daily papers as far afield as the USA, Australia, Singapore and even mainland China. Although there is widespread apathy towards the events of Christianity we should not forget the widespread latent interest. Recently I have been studying the date of the birth of Christ, and a paper on this is in its final stages of preparation. Again, it is difficult to be 100% certain, but the evidence points strongly to a particular year (and not to 25 December!). Perhaps this will be another piece placed correctly in the jigsaw of truth.

I have found, and continue to find, great intellectual satisfaction from both science and Christian belief. There is much we do not understand in both. There are many challenges. For example, do recent ideas about chaos have any relevance to free will? Upon re-reading this chapter I find that I have mainly concentrated on insights we can gain about Christianity from our knowledge of science. What about the reverse? I think the most important thing Christianity has taught me as a mechanistic scientist is not to lose my sense of wonder. What a brilliant creative genius God is to produce the universe and life in all its complexity, diversity and beauty, from a single small beginning. To a Christian, the heavens declare the glory of God.

10

Personal Faith and Commitment

Elizabeth Rhodes – Chemical engineer

Dr Elizabeth Rhodes, BSc, PhD.
Born 1930. Educated Penistone Grammar School, Bedford College (London University), Battersea Polytechnic, and Imperial College, London.
Former Lecturer in Chemical Engineering, University College, Swansea.
Warden of Mary Williams Hall, University College, Swansea, 1966–77.
Member of Council and Court of University College, Swansea, and Court of University of Wales since 1988.
Governing Body of Church in Wales since 1975.

'I know whom I have believed, and am persuaded that he is able to keep that which I have committed unto him against that day' (2 Tim 1:12). Time and again I come back to those words of St Paul as I realise my faith in Christ my Saviour is faltering amid the stresses of life. It was during my first year as an undergraduate at Bedford College that I committed my life to Christ. It was a gradual and a reasoned conviction, not emotional; I am a very self-contained person and try to keep my deepest feelings under control.

I am the eldest of four children but, owing to family circumstances and my own ill-health as a child, I lived with my mother's sister and her husband who had no children. I was very much on my own and spent a lot of time reading and building equipment and machines using Meccano and construction kits. When I grew older and fitter, I entered a coeducational grammar school about twelve miles away from where I lived. At school I was fascinated by chemistry and physics, and the desire grew to know how systems behaved and reacted. At this time, too, my interest in the creation of the universe and history of the world was aroused. In the early teens I was essentially an agnostic; though I knew the basic stories from the Bible, I dismissed the Old Testament stories as being in the same category as fairy tales. I admitted, however, that Jesus and the apostles in the New Testament were historical people. I did not know what to believe about the miracles but concluded that they could not be scientifically tested and hence could not have occurred.

In 1945 I matriculated with distinctions in nine subjects, and had to decide whether to choose a scientific career or become a historian. Science won because I wanted to make things happen and enjoyed the challenge to my understanding and practical ability. World War II had ended and the secrets of radar, jet engines, penicillin and the enormous, though fearsome, possibilities of nuclear power were revealed. I wanted to be in on the action and discovery; there seemed to be no limits to the possibilities of science.

On the other hand, the end of the war revealed the brutalities and savagery of the human race in the atrocities of Belsen and Auschwitz and the catastrophic damage of the nuclear bombs at Hiroshima and Nagasaki. I had seen the fires and destruction from the air raids on Sheffield, and though my immediate family escaped any war deaths, a cousin died soon after repatriation from a Japanese prisoner of war camp. Shortly, too, my aunt became ill with cancer and though surgery and radiotherapy were tried, it was not curable. She was a Christian and persuaded me towards the end of my school days to attend an adult confirmation class at the village church. The vicar did his best to help me, but though I knew that the scientific view of the world was not the whole truth, I still had many questions and doubts. At this time, as headgirl, it was my duty frequently to read the Bible passage at school assembly and this forced me to think carefully about the claims of Christ.

It was in this seeking frame of mind that I entered Bedford College in London. I think my aunt was praying for me because almost the first people I met belonged to the Christian Union or the Student Christian Movement; many have remained life-long friends. Most Sundays I attended the local Anglican church in Finchley Road, but occasionally I would go to the London Intervarsity Fellowship of Christian Unions (LIFCU) services at St Paul's, Portman Square, or St Peter's, Vere Street, and some of my questions of faith were answered. I reasoned that the critical question was the truth of the Resurrection of Christ, and reading the book *Who Moved the Stone?* by Frank Morison finally convinced me that Christ did rise from the dead, though in precisely what form I could only speculate. History is as important as science. I knew that scientific evidence of the fact of the Resurrection was unobtainable but I was prepared to believe the testimony of the apostles and the early church; and so I committed my life to Christ as my Saviour. I joined the Christian Union although I was not a frequent attender; I was too unsure of myself to be happy in prayer meetings or study groups, preferring the more structured and less personally committed framework of Anglican worship and teaching.

Failure and success

My initial two or three years as a Christian were an unhappy time. My aunt died at the end of my first year at university, and though I returned to the house to look after my uncle during the vacations I felt very alone. I did not see much of my parents and was not able to discuss my problems with them. I was also uncertain about the compatibility of a scientific career and Christian commitment, so that by the final year I had lost my enthusiasm and motivation to work for a degree in chemistry. This coupled with a bad bout of glandular fever meant that I failed my degree.

'Pride goes before a fall.' I had nearly always been first or second in my class at school and had entered Bedford with a college scholarship and been top of the class in the first year. I had to get away to think and sort out my priorities; I spent a month cycling and walking in the Scottish Highlands. I determined to go back and retake the final year. London University allowed me to register as an internal student at Battersea Polytechnic to resit the examination; a small legacy from my aunt helped me to afford to do so. It was during this year that I started to attend All Souls Church, Langham Place, which had just reopened with Dr John Stott as Rector. It was the teaching in this church that encouraged me to see the necessity for Christians to think through their faith to meet the challenges and interpretations of science. There was a need to have a reasoned and reasonable faith; Christ needed scientists as well as preachers and teachers.

Eventually, I gained a second class honours degree in chemistry and started work as a research and development chemist in an engineering firm manufacturing chipboard, and then at British Drug Houses. My original dreams of a research degree had been shattered by that failure in 1951, but perhaps God had different plans for me. I spent a summer cycling and walking in the Alps. On returning to work in London I rejoined All Souls Church and became involved in the youth club, missionary committee and Bible study groups. I shared a flat at various times with three former friends from the Bedford College Christian Union who were also working in London, and their friendship was a tremendous help to me. I joined the Research Scientists'

Christian Fellowship (now called Christians in Science) and was a regular participant in the London meetings and the annual conference. I was interested in geology, having taken this subject as part of my degree course, so the discussions on the origins of the universe, evolutionary theories and the biblical creation narratives were of particular help. I also attended a number of evening theological courses at the London Bible College so I began to understand the Bible better, and the Old Testament became more meaningful. I had badly needed teaching and instruction in the Christian faith, and those four years when I was not involved in academic work were vital.

Towards the end of this time I became dissatisfied with industrial research and development as I found the continual switches from unfinished projects most frustrating. I thought that overseas missionary work might be a possibility, but I was not trained as a teacher and my communication skills were better adapted to students than children, so that door did not open. I had started to take a part-time MSc research degree when a friend at All Souls heard about this and suggested I apply for a research contract postgraduate vacancy at Imperial College. This I did, and in early 1956 found myself trying to understand and start a spectroscopic project on the thermo-dynamics and melting phenomena of low melting alkali salts, under the supervision of Professor A.R. Ubbelohde.

This research contract was funded by a Defence Ministry; was I as a Christian prepared to work on this project? In the first instance, the project was not secret and the results would be publishable. Second, having grown up during World War II, I knew sufficient of the history of Europe in the twentieth century to be aware of the nearly fatal unpreparedness of Britain in the face of Nazi aggression. Third, my recent study of the historical books of the Old Testament had shown me that armed conflict might be part of God's plan in certain situations.

Those years were enjoyable; I had difficult practical and

theoretical problems to solve, an excellent research group and a stimulating supervisor. I was back on the academic track and this time successfully gained a highly commended PhD, the Lessing Medal of Imperial College, and the opportunity to present a research paper at the Royal Society. We had had a double breakthrough: the technical feat of obtaining the first spectral data of a molten salt at 300–400°C and a direct insight into the structure of a melt and the melting phenomena. Afterwards, I stayed at Imperial College as a senior research assistant in charge of the molten salt research group, under Professor Ubbelohde, with opportunities to publish further research papers and travel in Europe and the USA. For my last four years at Imperial College I was sub-warden at Beit Hall and involved in helping the women students at the college. I enjoyed sports such as hockey and tennis, squash and cricket, and met the undergraduates on both sporting and social occasions. I still continued as a member of All Souls Church and led Bible studies both there and at Imperial College.

Swansea: students, responsibilities and church life

However, it was time for a change and a new challenge. I had finally proved my academic ability, but it has never been easy for a woman to obtain full academic posts and there were limited opportunities in my research field in the UK. I felt that I should be more involved with people and, following on from my experience at Beit Hall, I started to look for an opening as a warden of a hall of residence where I could also have academic teaching duties. In the mid-sixties universities were expanding, and I was appointed as warden of a new hall for 200 women students on the campus of University College, Swansea, and a part-time lecturer in the Department of Chemical Engineering. I was particularly pleased to obtain this opportunity as it did not involve catering or housekeeping, since these were provided centrally for the three campus halls, the other two being men's halls. It was also agreed that I should have substantial teaching responsibilities for thermodynamics and certain applied chemistry aspects in the Chemical Engineering Department.

Now came some searching questions for my Christian faith. I was in a position of responsibility and inevitably what I did or did not do or say would be noticed and commented upon. I had to appoint staff in the hall, select the students who had applied for residence, and establish a reasonable regime and discipline in the hall. The wardens of the neighbouring men's halls and I kept rules to a minimum consistent with fire and safety regulations, ie, we needed to know who was in the hall after 11 pm as the halls were ten-storey blocks. I was happy to do this for morals are set by example and ethos, not by rules and regulations. In the seventies we suffered the ubiquitous student disruptions, and as warden I was very much in the firing-line, particularly as I thought that the permissive attitude had gone too far; freedom yes, but that freedom had to be modified by consideration for others. Then, after ten years, the campus halls became mixed and the wardens' appointments were terminated, so I made a sideways move to a full-time lectureship in chemical engineering, taking over the jobs of undergraduate admissions tutor and eventually first year course co-ordinator.

I joined St Paul's Church, Sketty, the nearest of the Anglican Churches in Wales. Initially I was not an active church member as time was limited with both hall and departmental duties; when I left hall I had time to participate more fully. I was elected to the governing body of the Church in Wales and also to the Parish Church Council. I have served in a number of capacities, eg, as a member of the Provincial Selection Board for Ministry, Partners in Mission Consultation, the Liturgical Revision Committee for the Eucharist, the Bishops' Advisory

Committee for Reorganisation of the Swansea Deanery, and currently as a member of the Diocesan Patronage Board. One of my greatest pleasures, however, was to help establish local Bible study groups in St Paul's and the ecumenical Sketty Council of Churches. In 1989 I represented the Council of Churches for Wales at a Conference on Faith and the Environment at Canterbury, where I provided technical input for the workshop on energy.

Hall and departmental teaching limited my time for research at Swansea so I concentrated on the uses of molten salts as heat transfer fluids and in fuel cells. Energy efficiency is important to the chemical engineer, and the ever-growing concern over the depletion of the world's nonrenewable energy resources and the greenhouse effect emphasises the need for research in this field. God lays on humanity the task of caring for his creation (Ps 8:6; Gen 1:26), yet we are so wasteful and misuse the world's resources. Virtually all the products and conveniences of the developed world require the use of nonrenewable energy, from the basic necessities such as food, heat and light to transport, refrigerators and television. In the mid-eighties interest increased in fuel cell research as worries grew about the depletion of fossil fuels and the massive amount of carbon dioxide produced from the combustion of carbon containing fuels.

Another project I started was the electrochemical removal of toxic chemicals from effluent streams, and I was asked to lecture in Madras, India. Visiting India made me very aware of the poverty of so many people and the desperate need for accessible technology. My Indian hosts at the Electrochemical Research Centre in Karaikudi showed us not only the advanced technical work they were doing but also how they were helping local village communities to improve and provide clean water supplies. I also visited university women's groups in Madras and Bangalore, and saw some of the work among women and children in education and the alleviation of poverty.

At this time I became increasingly concerned with the importance of alternative technology, technology transfer and the need to involve women in all aspects of technology, especially in underdeveloped countries. This was reinforced when I represented the Wales Assembly of Women at the Non-Governmental Organisations Forum at the United Nations Decade for Women Conference in Nairobi, Kenya. Most impressive was the impact of the African Women's Christian Organisations and their concern that young women should receive appropriate technological education. Increasingly I have become involved in promoting the access of women to education in science and engineering. Christ saved all humanity, and women, with their awareness of the needs of others and concern for the environment, need to be technologically educated to use their talents.

Choices and priorities

To summarise, I would say that my life experience has consisted of various stages, each dominated by different priorities; switches being governed by factors such as health, opportunities and a conviction that God wanted me to be in a particular place or to do a certain task. There have been a number of conflicts and no decision has been easy.

Initially, and most traumatic, was the conflict over pursuing a scientific career and Christian commitment; intellectual pride and acknowledgement of God's sovereignty were incompatible. I had to discover the hard way that God requires obedience first, and only then can he use you.

Direct conflict between my Christian faith and the particular fields of physical sciences and technology I am interested in have been minimal. In fact, my Christian faith has reinforced my interest in thermodynamics and electro-chemistry and the possibilities of promoting energy efficient systems and improving the environment. All energy resources (even renewable resources such as wind power) have disadvantages and may not be as environmentally benign as once thought. Nuclear power is potentially world destroying, but so may be carbon dioxide emissions from coal-burning power stations and transport vehicles.

The demands on my Christian love and commitment while running a hall of residence in the permissive seventies were high. I was continually under stress, especially when the hall became mixed; though the majority of students were supportive, the few who were not caused a lot of trouble, so I was glad to relinquish my appointment when the college reorganised the halls. A continual conflict is that of allocation of time. In hall, in a caring role, I needed to spend time talking with students and staff, yet the administration had to be done efficiently, lectures and laboratories prepared carefully, student work marked and research projects supervised, all to the best of my ability as a professing Christian. After leaving hall my evenings were free, but I now had major departmental administrative duties. However, I was able to increase church commitment despite looking after my home and garden.

A difficulty has always been that I am a woman in a predominantly male profession. Even though about 10 per cent of engineering undergraduates are women, there are relatively few women in academic posts in general, and for twenty years I was the only woman lecturer out of seventy staff in the engineering faculty. There are particular tensions for women in such situations and I accumulated a number of time-consuming tasks as I tried to be reliable and conscientious. I believe that it is part of Christian witness to participate fully in college and other activities, and sometimes these conflict with career development, but I feel that it has probably been God's will for me to move in such directions rather than spend a lot of time on research. I have certainly found that the opportunities which have occurred in meeting and teaching students, especially women, from many parts of the world, and also in travel have deepened my Christian faith.

Pathways

Roger Bolton – Industrial chemist

Dr Roger G. Bolton, MA, D Phil.
Born 1946. Educated Leeds Modern School and New College, Oxford.
Head of Regulatory Affairs Group, Zeneca since 1984.
Accredited local preacher in the Methodist Church since 1970.

Some may ask what a chemist who has spent almost twenty years in industry, the majority in product development rather than primary research, can offer to a collection of ideas relating our faith to real science. My answer would be that the broader issues into which I have been plunged as a result of my involvement in projects associated with the development of new drugs have given me particular opportunities to consider how science fits in a divinely created world.

Life is an exploration for all of us; from the earliest age we learn chiefly by our experiences. God's gift of the means to record and accumulate information, and to communicate and transfer important facts, adds an extra dimension to our learning ability without in any way lessening the need for experience. A scientist is given the training to be able to use and learn from his experiences in an objective manner. Is our scientific training a help or a hindrance in our earthly pilgrimage?

I frequently wish that I had a humanities background so that I could better understand the historical, cultural and philosophical context of biblical truth. It is an open question whether competence in linguistics, philosophy or ancient history serves the Christian better than scientific training. Does the student of literature have the edge when attempting to understand the truth of God's word? After all, we tend to enter that field of study which first took our enthusiasm and which captured our interest at the critical age for options; are we hindered in our Christian life by our adolescent choices? Perhaps the answer is that our own particular expertise sets a foundation on which other skills can be developed in a complementary manner, giving each of us our unique perspective.

There are many pathways in life, not all of which lead to good destinations; some are recorded for us simply as pictures of routes that we have not or never will experience. The important thing is that we each have our own experience, and this is, in part at least, the result of learning from our mistakes, however much we strive to shape our way in accordance with what we believe to be right. For myself, I find it helpful, in following the path that Jesus described, to have also a glimpse of our exploration of the physical world; a scientific training is a privilege, opening an opportunity to appreciate man's best attempts to understand God's creation. So my testimony is of two paths, down which I travel falteringly; one records my discovery of my own faith and the other amplifies that faith in my perception of the physical world. There is nothing unique in this; such an analysis will be familiar to many in their own lives. Of course, we make mistakes or false turnings on both paths due to our inadequate training or understanding, but these in themselves can be necessary lessons to restore our perspective or refer us back to that part of our understanding which is secure. We share with many when we overstretch ourselves and wrongly leap ahead of the truth.

Experience

As a teenager I was introduced to the writings of Père Teilhard de Chardin who had shocked his Jesuit establishment by espousing evolutionary views consistent with his palaeontological studies. This led him to his mystical concept of an 'Omega Point' and a perception that creation is a continuing work of God, a remaining presence and not a completed piece of history. As a consequence of such readings I was introduced to a vision of life as a journey of both discovery and mission, in which each individual has to learn new things and to leave the world changed as a result of having been there—an allegory of the uncertainty principle to which I shall return.

A vivid recollection of my university days is of two series of lectures given in the unusual location of the lecture theatre of the University Museum in Oxford. I say 'unusual' because almost all regular teaching was done within the departments themselves, but the old museum had an enormous auditorium which could be used if large numbers were expected.

Charles Coulson, who was Rouse Ball Professor of Applied Mathematics, used to give a foundation course in wave mechanics to a very broad group of undergraduates reading physics, mathematics, chemistry and engineering. His ability to make this abstruse subject come together and make sense was admirably displayed in his books, but even more so in his lectures, which were de rigeur for all of us. But this was the same Charles Coulson, Vice-President of the Methodist Conference, who opened his home (within a week or two of our arrival in Oxford) to those of us who were freshers from Methodist churches. He saw no contradiction between this and the development of his mathematics into a fundamental understanding of the nature of matter; his modelling of atomic structure displayed the beauty and symmetry we expect of God's creation. From that time I began to appreciate the benefits of being able both to understand man's insight into the world and have an awareness of God's purpose and guiding hand.

During my research years we were privileged to have Melvin Calvin as a visiting professor in the university for a year. Nobel Laureate for his studies into the mechanism of photosynthesis, he was focusing then on 'Chemical Evolution'. The wide appeal of his work meant that his series of lectures were also delivered before audiences of several hundred in the museum. His description of mass-spectrometric studies of oil shales did not devalue my appreciation of creation: on the contrary, it served to whet my appetite to continue the exploration of the true extent of the wonder.

Testimony

There is not necessarily a fundamental conflict between the scientific and the religious mind; indeed, both ought to have similar features—a combination of critical reasoning with a measure of inspiration. Probably none of the fundamental discoveries that have changed established thought have come from the hard slog of routine scientific detective work; the great advances in science all spring from minds prepared through careful and painstaking observation and thus enabled to make a leap forward in thinking. When tested by experiment, this vision is confirmed to the satisfaction of the peer group.

Scientific advance needs a firm foundation in fundamental principles and in general these are learned with the help of models, which consolidate their conceptualisation. For example, it is usual to learn wave mechanics after simple quantum theory, and that in turn after some simplistic 'billiard-ball' representation of atomic and molecular structure. Scientific modelling is a broad-based pyramid and employs basic skills. So in my Christian life I have found that lasting commitment must be based on sound scriptural knowledge and an active prayer-life if the mountain-top experiences of inspiration are not to fade away. The presence of the Holy Spirit is personally real to everyone at certain times, but the individual can only witness to that Spirit in his or her life when we build on its gifts with the facilities God has provided. Christ came into my life most clearly as a teenager at a large evangelistic mission, but the Holy Spirit was able to take a mind prepared by a childhood exposure to Methodism and use a gifted counsellor in follow-up who introduced me to the means of grace—a great blessing and strength subsequently.

The molecular sciences have given me an awareness of the properties of matter which enhances for me the wonder of God's creation. Who cannot marvel at the manner in which complex molecular structures can be understood in terms of orbitals obeying simple rules of symmetry? The routine study of biosynthetic pathways whetted my appetite to study applications relevant to biological systems. To see the elegant radiolabelled studies which established the origins of complex polyisoprenoids in acetate residues is to recognise a divine work of beauty. The study of living systems reveals the miracles of structural chemistry and exquisitely balanced thermodynamic relationships which are concealed from the observer at a macroscopic level. As each new revelation is made, the subtleties of enzymically-induced molecular reactivity have enhanced my confidence that such biochemical mechanisms are no chance artefact: they are a vital part of that complex, highly adaptable self-supporting system of energetics which is a living organism. I perceive in Darwin's empirical observations another indication of the wonder of creation by God's continuing and guiding hand.

Having been fortunate to be able to develop broad interests rather than a narrow academic speciality, I have been encouraged to find that they have been mutually reinforcing. In his book *The Tao of Physics,* Frijtof Capra bemoans the absence of mysticism in Western philosophy and draws attention to the contradictions in seeking a wholly mechanical approach to sub-atomic structure. He cites the Heisenberg uncertainty principle as an example of this. (For any unfamiliar with it, the principle says that as soon as anyone looks into the atom to measure an electron you change its energy; it is impossible to describe both the energy and the position of an electron at the same time.) This led me to think again of Professor Coulson. In his theological lectures and writings he rejected a 'God in the gaps' in which God is imported like the proverbial US Cavalry merely to deal with the inexplicable. I believe that glimpses of fundamental order and design which God-given scientific insight has revealed are wholly consistent with a Bible-based awareness of order and design in creation. As with both God's revelation in Scripture and with our scientific exploration, it is the search for overall understanding which is more important than the discussion and analysis of every full stop and comma. Or in reverse, the great experimentalists support their hypotheses not by an all-embracing comprehensive modelling of the macro-system but by the unequivocal display of one or more key facets through cleverly designed experiments.

This is surely what the scientist who is a Christian must share with his non-scientific brethren; just as Crick and Watson needed only to confirm the existence of an α–helix crystallographically before describing the double-stranded DNA chain, so it is wholly inappropriate to expect Scripture to be a rigorously reasoned case in the twentieth-century sense for God's presence in the world and its origins. Instead, we must surely see the Bible as the divinely inspired source of records of God's hand at work, and which, to the person who has real faith, constitutes the independent observations that support our own witness. Thus I submit that there are immense parallels between 'real science' and 'real faith', for each has much to encourage the other. Just as the origins of both science and formal education in Europe were in the Christian church, so today the synergy and complementarity of the scientific mind and the religious mind is evident.

Difficulties

It probably appears that all the above is very rosy and simplistic, and in fairness I have to share also the difficulties that I have experienced, and my perception of the conflicts between science and faith.

Although we have received great benefits from science and technology, I am often aware that we rely excessively on material things. So we seek to bleed the planet dry of its natural resources, we treat the oceans as dumping grounds, and corrupt useful discoveries into instruments of domination or greed. Is this a consequence of the over-application of science as the key to unlock natural wealth? Have we taken our search for gain too far or is it just that we know too many examples of excesses? Certainly, former British Prime Minister Harold Wilson's 'technological revolution' has taken place. His speech which set forth the science education boom of the sixties predated the micro-chip, lunar landings, recombinant-DNA technology and digital data-recording. Yet despite these exciting advances, we are witnessing a drift away from science in schools. A significant factor in the failure of the dream to hold must be the perception that science and technology have led man-kind into greedy and destructive ways. Happily, science also offers the means of fighting back against the consequences of these excesses; we must encourage our scientific disciplines to improve the environment and support better stewardship of natural resources.

It would be dishonest to pretend that I do not frequently seek to rationalise improperly many biblical events. As a practical scientist one is encouraged to be solution-orientated, and valid though many of my rationalisations may be, we must still recognise that it doesn't matter whether an earthquake did assist Joshua to bring down the walls or freak cross-winds could have parted the Red Sea. Human ingenuity has published many a theory that fits facts well and yet is wholly erroneous. Does it matter whether all or none of the miracles can be explained physically? If all are explicable or all are beyond explanation there would still be those who would claim God is an unsupportable myth and others who would argue that God can operate only through the established mechanisms of the physical world. Both positions are of course wrong since our God transcends human understanding and displays his power generously in excess of the recorded biblical miracles. Remember St Paul's words on the foolishness of human wisdom and the stumbling-block of the cross (1 Cor 1:18–25).

As well as intellectual difficulties, it is clear that there can be significant clashes of faith with the cutting edges of our various disciplines. Typical of these is the embryo research debate in which a recognition of God's loving hand is claimed by both sides. It is undeniable that life itself is already present in the fused gametes well before any recognisable cell-differentiation can be identified as signifying the start of uniquely *human* life. But, with the tools we now have available, there is every scientific and moral reason to conduct experiments towards the correction of genetic defects. Our resolution of such conflicts frequently depends less on objective criteria than on our preconceptions. The parents of wholly healthy children may be inclined to join with those who cherish a severely congenitally handicapped offspring in condemning the destruction of the embryo for experimentation. On the other hand, an expectant parent, or the exhausted guardian of a severely incapacitated child may associate with the infertile couple in rating most highly the investigation of genetic disorders. Whose is the greater love towards the life of the world? The one clear view I can take is that the least objective group is that whose research reputation depends on the availability of human embryos.

Undoubtedly, the future holds many challenges for the Christian who is also a scientist, especially in the areas of cell biology. The reconciliation of disparate views of what constitutes 'life' and 'human life' will continue to exercise many. The application of modern biotechnology to mammalian cells will raise serious questions of ethics and belief.

In dealing with such questions, it is important for all of us to be aware of opposing views. Useful applications of modern biotechnology are likely to be marred if cell biologists are deaf to the opinions of those who sincerely hold a seemingly conflicting perception of the nature of human life. Conversely, any assessment of the theological correctness of proposals for research in this area must be based on careful exegesis and not on a stylised collection of extracted scriptural verses. To challenge constructively is to raise the quality of debate to the greater profit of us all; we have a responsibility in debate for trying to ensure that opposing views neither stagnate nor develop into an unjustifiable obsession. Ultimately, the assessment for the Christian must be governed by biblical truth, but the search for a proper understanding will be enhanced by the challenges of the new science.

In conclusion, then, it seems to me that, just as God has given those gifted in the arts, literature and music the ability to strike new heights in expressing their perception of God, so the scientist can bring to mankind a deeper and richer understanding of God's revelation in creation. Creation is so wonderful that it would be wrong to say that it should not be investigated. To behave thus invites the condemnation of the servant who buried the funds left him in trust because he was afraid of what might go wrong (Mt 25:14–30). Surely we should try to understand better the world and the living things in it. To do so will be to take on a great responsibility for behaving with integrity, and it is here that the dialogue between the Christian and the scientist is really critical. Just as physicists require standards of mass, length and time on which to base the measurement and modelling of the physical world, so all of us have need of an eternal reference standard against which to judge the ethics of our work, a yardstick to measure our pathway.

12

Brains, Mind and Faith

Malcolm Jeeves – Psychologist

Professor Malcolm A. Jeeves, CBE, MA, PhD, FBPsS, FRSE.
Born 1926. Educated Stamford School and St John's College, Cambridge.
Hon Research Professor of Psychology, St Andrew's University since 1993.
Professor of Psychology, 1969–93 (Vice-Principal 1981–85), Director, Medical Research Council Cognitive Neuroscience Research Group, 1984–89.
Previously Professor of Psychology, Adelaide University, 1959–69.
Vice-President, Royal Society of Edinburgh, 1990–93.
Member, Science and Engineering Research Council, 1985–89.
Medical Research Council, 1984–88.
Honorary Sheriff, Fife, from 1986.
Formerly President IVF (Australia) and UCCF (UK).

It's not always easy to be a psychologist and a Christian. Some aspects of psychological theory in general and the psychology of religion in particular make one wary of accepting beliefs at their face value. They can also alert one to motives for beliefs other than, or in addition to, those ostensibly given. Wishful thinking, for example, is always ready to influence beliefs of many kinds, not just religious ones. And as psychologists, we can certainly marshall an impressive catalogue of psychological mechanisms to 'explain away' someone else's beliefs or justify our own.

Some of the most widely published psychological accounts of how and why religious beliefs arise in the first place (like William Sargant's 'brain washing'), and how they function for us (like Sigmund Freud's 'escape mechanisms'), have sufficient credibility to provide ready-made rationalisations for being sceptical about some of the more extravagant claims made in the name of religion. As a consequence I have become doubtful about taking testimonies at their face value and correspondingly hesitant when asked to give my own. It is sad to recall eloquent and moving professions of personal Christian commitment based on apparently convincing personal experiences, only to discover later that some of those concerned will now have nothing to do with the Christian faith. This cautions me never to forget how vulnerable may be my own faith—and yet the same thought brings home even more convincingly, after nearly fifty years as a Christian, how unchanging and unfailing is God's love, and how boundless is his grace—his totally unmerited care and kindness to me. And that for me is the heart of the matter—God's unfailing and unchanging love. Having brought me to personal faith in him in my teens, God has made himself more and more real down the years, whether as a young infantry officer in Germany in the 1940s, or through university as an undergraduate and research student at Cambridge, or throughout a university career as Professor of Psychology, first in Australia, and now at St Andrews in Scotland. Over the years it is his care above all which stands out.

Some continuing puzzles

Wishful thinking and all that

The impact of psychology on Christian faith differs in some respects from that of other sciences. It raises questions about the very nature and function of religious—including Christian—beliefs, before one ever gets to the content of specific beliefs, such as the nature of man. Are religious beliefs, of whatever kind, it asks, nothing but wish-fulfilments or escape mechanisms? Why do people need religious beliefs? How do they function?

Psychologists have studied almost every aspect of the religious life—conversion, prayer, spiritual growth, church membership. And there is much to learn and to make us uncomfortable as the psychological spotlight is turned on our beliefs and behaviour. But nothing emerges that should surprise us, assuming we have taken seriously the unflattering picture of ourselves so graphically and eloquently portrayed in Scripture. On the one hand, we are in some profound sense made in the image of God, our Father Creator; and yet we are never, never allowed to forget that we are of the earth, earthy. There are dramatic reminders of this in the lives of the great heroes of the faith, who so often sink to depths of disobedience matched only by the heights of their spiritual experience and sacrificial obedience.

Psychologising about what religious beliefs do for the individual or the group has a history that stretches at least as far back as the Day of Pentecost. Then the behaviour of the first Christians was attributed to the effect of wine. For Freud, religious belief was illusory; it was simply wishful thinking. If you want to avoid taking Christianity or any other religion seriously, Freud can help you. Even though on close inspection both his data and his arguments are dubious, they still possess enough truth for all of us to pause and ask whether we may not at times be exploiting our religious beliefs. Who of us is free from the tendency to indulge in just a little wishful thinking about what we might receive or achieve through our religious beliefs, our prayers, our religious practices?

Arguments like Freud's, however, turn out to be two-edged swords. The Dutch philosopher, Rümke, combined Freud's assumptions with what was known of Freud's early life, and showed how on his own theory Freud should seek to get rid of the idea of a Father God and of religion. That kind of psychologising can never help decide whether the great events of redemption history happened or what they meant. Nothing in Freud's writings can tell us whether there was a people of Israel, a Moses or a David, an exodus from Egypt, a man Jesus Christ or whether he rose from the dead, or indeed whether there was a small frightened band of first believers who turned the world upside down. None of those things can be settled by psychologising, using Freud's brand or any other. To find that out we must ask what and where is the relevant evidence claimed to support those beliefs. Then we must go and study it for ourselves and be open to meeting the 'One Who Is' if he reveals himself.

Man: scientific and Christian

Psychology and its associated discipline of neuroscience raises searching questions about human nature. For example, almost every advance in neuropsychology and neuroscience over the last twenty years has seemed to tighten the link between mental life and brain processes. And yet it still seems natural for us as Christians to talk about having a 'soul', which, in some undefined way, inhabits our body and departs at physical death. How is that possible in view of the way that psychology and neuroscience emphasise our psychophysical unity? The common pew-dwellers' view of man implies a soul or mind inhabiting a body. How do we resolve this conflict?

Evidence for the tightening of the mind/brain link comes from several directions, and, in particular, from studying how mental life changes when the brain is damaged. Thus a patient may complain that whereas he has no difficulty recognising motor cars or household objects, he can no longer recognise faces, even his own and those of his close relatives. Using modern imaging techniques it emerges that such a patient invariably has damage to particular parts of his brain. Further work, using the techniques of single-cell recording in the brains of alert and awake animals, has identified particular columns of cells which seem to fire only when presented with a particular face. Thus the tightness of the mind/brain link becomes more impressive with every advance in neuroscience.

It is impertinent, if not risky, for a mere psychologist to hold forth on a Christian view of man, a topic on which there are countless volumes of theological writings. But if I am to say anything about some of the puzzles raised by psychology and neuroscience I must first say what I see as the salient features of the biblical account. They are as follows. First, a timeless view, saying relevant and important things throughout history, prescientific and scientific alike. That alone should warn against misconstruing it or its vocabulary by endowing it, in the late twentieth century, with a precision never intended. Second, the Bible emphasises our relation to God; it is not concerned with a scientific analysis of human beings. Third, what the Bible has to say about man is given so that ordinary men and women can live daily to the glory of God; it does not offer information to help construct twentieth-century psychological models of humankind. Fourth, the language of the Bible is not the language of any particular ancient or modern experimental science. The Bible does not talk about species, but about people; it is not biological but biographical. It is not interested in the physiological, biochemical or psychological properties of human beings (in the late twentieth-century sense), but in the actions of men and women in history. Fifth, the Bible is a library of books; as such, different writers give different emphases to common themes and thus enrich the whole.

With these guidelines we discover a broad-based picture of man in Scripture. It highlights his physical make-up: he must remember he is of the earth, earthy. He has a capacity for mental life and he is able to make moral decisions, including an appreciation of the spiritual dimension to life. When these aspects work harmoniously together they help maintain a personal relationship with God and with other people. And the relationship with God is an enduring one. It will continue through the transition of physical death and guarantees an identifiable embodiment in a glorified body after physical death and decay. Today we know ourselves and each other through our psycho-physical embodiment; in some mysterious and profound sens- we shall, so our Christian faith assures us, continue to know and be known in a new and glorified embodiment 'in that day'.

Attempts to try to 'fit' the latest psychological model of man to the biblical picture, however well meaning, are not to be encouraged. Not only do they misunderstand what the scientific models are about, they also reveal a mis-understanding of the purposes of the Christian teaching about man. Scientific models of man, by their nature, remain silent on questions of good and evil, sin, redemption, and eternal life—issues which are central to the Christian view of man.

The need for multiple levels of investigation

I work in the sub-discipline of neuropsychology and the thing that impresses me most is that in order to do justice to the complexity of even the simplest aspects of mind, we need to study simultaneously and concurrently several different levels. We take for granted a hierarchy of levels. We work at the biophysical level, the biochemical level, the level of single-cell functioning, the level of groups of cells functioning together. We work at the level of systems within the brain, we work in terms of neural nets, we work in terms of psychological categories. And it is stupid to spend time searching for gaps in the explanation given at one level in order to fit in an explanation at another level. The way to an integrated understanding of man is not to hunt for gaps in any particular scientific picture so that we can fit in other entities, whether it be the soul or whatever, but to explore how the accounts at the different levels are related. It is not that we translate what is happening at one level into what is happening at another. The descriptions we give at the different levels are complementary, not identical or independent.

A reductionist approach insists that ultimately our scientific account must be in terms of physical forces between molecules, and leads us to deny freedom of choice, the most common of all experiences. Accounts at other levels by physiologists, psychologists or theologians are seen as merely temporary expedients, acceptable only until a full account is available at the molecular level. Everything else ultimately will become superfluous.

Such an approach, with its underlying presuppositions, is now generally recognised as being both philosophically misguided and scientifically unproductive. Roger Sperry, a Nobel prize-winner in brain science, wrote recently, 'The consciousness revolution of the 1970s can be seen to represent a renunciation by a major scientific discipline of the reductionist "quantum mechanics philosophy" which had previously dominated scientific thinking.' The philosopher, Michael Polanyi, has pointed out that explanations in terms of molecules only have, by their nature, no concepts even for the function of the parts being described.

In this regard the familiar example of a computer solving mathematical problems is helpful. We may describe the activity of a computer in terms of molecules, the motions of physical particles or in terms of integrated circuits, but the mathematician would energetically assert that such accounts do not convey the understanding that he, the mathematician, has of the computer's essential activity from his point of view. Thus it is possible for an explanation to be complete in its own terms but not to render superfluous another explanation given at a different level. I find computer analogies of this kind most helpful in trying to relate mind talk and brain talk, both of which are essential in cognitive neuroscience research.

Faith: help or hindrance?

From time to time events or people have a disproportionate effect on one's thinking. For me such an occasion was in the early 1950s when I heard Professor R. Hooykaas, of the Free University of Amsterdam, lecture in Cambridge on 'Philosophia Libera: Christian Faith and the Freedom of Science'. Later expanded into his bestselling book, *Religion and the Rise of Science,* Hooykaas' lecture put the present debates between science and faith in a firm historical context, showing in an exciting and convincing way the true freedom that is both the birthright of every Christian and also that which frees me as a scientist to pursue my career with enthusiasm and energy. He pointed out how the early scientists discarded rationalistic pretensions. Reason was not their goal; it could be used to criticise as well as to erect deductive systems. They realised that science does not lead to absolute truth, but is essentially the result of applying a particular methodological approach to studying what Hooykaas called 'divine revelation manifest in nature'. Openness to follow the evidence where it leads was a hallmark of the great scientists of the past. It should also be characteristic of every Christian committed to evidence rather than popular or transient interpretations based on rationalistic prejudices; that very liberating attitude remains for me an instrinsic part of the Christian faith.

There are, however, times when one's Christian faith may not seem a help and can be quite unsettling in producing real puzzles. For example, there is the enduring mismatch between what we profess and what we actually do and are. The apostle Peter, despite his protestations of loyalty 'even unto death', was soon denying any association with his Lord; Thomas, despite his beliefs, was at times full of doubt; the early disciples, despite the reality of their experience and their readiness to suffer, found that they were still human and could all too readily fall into quarrelling among themselves; Paul complained that 'I do not understand my own actions. For I do not do what I want . . . but the evil I do not want is what I do' (Rom 7:15, 19).

It has seemed to me that recently we have, at times, become so infected by ever more extravagant claims from advertisers and the media that something similar has infected our Christian thought and actions, though without any biblical warrant. In some Christian circles excessive, and unbiblical claims are made for what your faith 'can do for you'. Being a Christian becomes a free ticket to a combined heavenly supermarket and magic show.

At times I have found myself in church on a Sunday morning singing hymns which affirm the reality of our trust in God. But standing on the pavement outside when the service is over I hear some of those who were singing with me with such tremendous enthusiasm, conviction and perhaps accompanying bodily movements, speaking as if all that belonged only to inside the church. Somehow they are living in two worlds; somehow the singing of the words of the hymns does not escape into the world outside. There is, as I have already said, nothing new in this. But the contrast becomes stark because of the exaggerated claims. Why mimic the world and its pretentious exaggerations? Our God was incarnate. He was tired, lonely, at times bewildered, so why shouldn't we be? What can we do, I ask myself, to bring out persistently and emphatically the underlying theme of Scripture that this is *one* world, our Father's world, *not two* worlds. Here surely some of the things written by psychologists, both unbelieving and believing, about how religious beliefs and religious practices can become 'wishful thinking' receives unsolicited support. We all have a long way to go to learn the reality of true discipleship. We fool no one but ourselves by making exaggerated, unsubstantiated claims for our faith.

Faith and science—a mutual benefit

The lecture by Professor Hooykaas I mentioned earlier contained a quotation from a seventeenth-century scientist, Nathaniel Carpenter. He wrote, 'I am free, I am bound by nobody's word, except to those inspired by God; if I oppose these in the least degree, I beseech God to forgive me my audacity of judgement, as I have been moved not so much by longing for some opinion of my own as by my love for the freedom of science.' I still find Carpenter's words helpful.

The task of properly relating what we discover about the creation through science with what we learn about it in Scripture is a continuing one. And we are, according to Scripture, an intrinsic part of the physical creation, 'of the earth, earthy', 'from dust to dust'. We come neither to our science nor to the interpretation of the Bible free from presuppositions. Every perspective has its own preconceptions. Psychological research has confirmed over and over again what we know from our common experience, that the particular perspective we adopt influences what we see and how we react. To be aware of the ever-present influence of our presuppositions can help in part to free us from bondage to them.

I think the influence of presuppositions is particularly evident when Christians disagree over what the Bible is saying. If we come to Scripture with presuppositions from our scientific endeavours, we shall probably misread what we find; Scripture was written long before science, as we know it today, was ever thought of. Even so, down the centuries the same words have spoken clearly and powerfully to each generation. If, in our search to understand man and his nature, we recognise the difference between what is written for our learning in Scripture and what we discover in our scientific research, we shall be well set to avoid fruitless conflicts. But I suspect that we shall continue to witness attempts to read late twentieth-century scientific views of man into the words of Scripture. If only we could accept Scripture for what it is and let it speak for itself, we could gain so much and avoid so many unnecessary time-consuming and energy-draining debates and conflicts.

Looking at the scientific horizon in my own research I can see how puzzles about the relation between mind and brain will continue to fascinate and engross us for years to come. This means that we shall need to go on thinking through what we learn from our science about the tightening link between mind and brain and this will make it even more important, I believe, to recognise increasingly the Hebrew-Christian emphasis on psychophysical or somato-psysical unity. I am enthusiastic about my science and I believe that developments within psychology and neuro-science will lead on to discoveries which can be applied to the alleviation, and perhaps in some cases cure of the suffering that occurs when the brain, the physical substrate of the mind, is malfunctioning or diseased. Together with my humanist colleagues and those of other religious per-suasions I, as a Christian, can work enthusiastically with the added assurance that in so doing I am obeying my Father's command to subdue and be a good steward of the created order which includes man himself, made 'of the dust of the earth' but mysteriously also made 'in the image of God'.

13

Man—Dust with a Destiny

Monty Barker – Psychiatrist

Dr Montagu G. Barker, MB, ChB, FRCPEd, FRCPsych, DPM.
Educated Hutchesons' School, Glasgow, and St Andrew's University.
Consultant Psychiatrist in Bristol and Clinical Lecturer, Department of Mental Health, University of Bristol, since 1968.
Regional Postgraduate Tutor in Psychiatry for South West England.
External Advisor to the Selection School for Candidates to the Ministry of the Church of Scotland.

Scientism

My early training in the 1960s was marked by the recent discovery and development of the new tranquillisers and antidepressants which, added to electroconvulsive therapy, benefited—and continue to benefit—patients with severe mental illness, however misused such treatments may sometimes be. There seemed to be a new breakthrough in 'scientific psychiatry' which could reduce all psychic suffering to genetic predisposition and abnormal brain physiology, for there was now a physical treatment which could 'cure'. Some of the most vigorous exponents of this approach wrote highly popular texts, such as Dr William Sargant's *Battle for the Mind*. In his book, Dr Sargant equated brain and mind, and all mental (including religious) experiences were reduced to physiological reactions. His physiology and psychology were severely criticised and rejected by many scientists, but his general equation of mental and spiritual experiences remained unassailed by the same scientific world.

My own training was in a school of psychiatry which professed rigorous exploration of all aspects of a patient's physical, mental and social development before assessment and treatment. But I was intrigued to discover that although careful histories were demanded on upbringing, sexual development, relationships and employment, the patient's goals in life and religious beliefs (or lack of them) rarely merited a mention; the failure of a doctor to elicit such information was never criticised. Even less attention was paid to the significance of such belief or lack of it in terms of how persons conducted their lives, unless the presenting symptoms and distress were expressed in specifically religious terminology.

As a trainee psychiatrist I became aware that most of my senior colleagues would seek only the clinical symptoms of their patients and ignore attitudes and value systems, viewing these as entirely personal matters not to be explored by the psychiatrist. A few would take a direct and usually hostile approach, tending automatically to blame strongly held religious views as being at least partly causal of a patient's illness. My interest in these matters provoked an invitation to review the subject of 'Religion and Psychiatry' at the weekly postgraduate meeting. By the mid-sixties, there had been only one major paper on the subject of religion and psychiatric illness in the fifty-year history of the leading British psychiatric journal; and that paper seemed to have been included only because it was a special guest lecture traditionally published in the journal each year. My own thesis was that a truly scientific approach within psychiatry could occur only where the patient's beliefs and goals, religious or otherwise, were explored along with the whole life situation. Everyone lives in accordance with some belief, whether expressed in religious terms or not, and to neglect the significance of this within a patient's life reduces that person in some way and makes him or her less than human.

Thirty years on the materialist and determinist bias to the understanding of psychiatric illness still has its followers. In an academic meeting exploring various approaches to understanding and treating depressed patients, a leading academic psychiatrist recently declared that he preferred to see patients as 'biological organisms predisposed by their genetic inheritance and subjected to certain life events'. The organic factors and the events affecting a patient's life were looked upon as legitimate subjects for study, but the person's own beliefs and the framework within which he understood and ordered life and events were looked upon as irrelevant.

It is an attitude dissected by Richard Holloway, now the Bishop of Edinburgh, when he wrote:

> This is my dilemma. . . . I am dust and ashes, frail and wayward, a set of predetermined behavioural responses, pro-grammed by my genetic inheritance and by social context, riddled with fears, beset with needs whose origins I do not understand and whose satisfaction I cannot achieve, quintescence of dust, and unto dust I shall return. Who can expect much of that?

But he went on to say:

> There is something else in me; there is an awareness that, truly, I am not what I am; and what I am and what I am not is what I truly am. Dust I may be, but troubled dust, dust that dreams, dust that has strange premonitions of transfiguration, of a glory in store, a destiny prepared, an inheritance that one day will be my own.

Relativism

These words reflect a change of emphasis that has taken place in the psychiatric profession. A new generation of psychiatrists, nurtured in the swinging sixties and influenced by a growing interest in 'consciousness', 'awareness' and 'spiritual' values, began to search for 'personal growth, character transformation, psychological rebirth and even mystical experience'. Physical methods of treating psychiatric illness and even the diagnostic categories of traditional psychiatry were severely criticised. By the 1970s there was a burgeoning of 'talking treatments', more technically known as psychotherapies and counselling programmes. Where Bishop Holloway had sought to direct his hearers to that longing for God the Creator innate in the hearts of all men, the new therapists offered fuller understanding and 'self-actualisation' through an ever-increasing number of psychotherapy programmes. One American writer spoke of the seventies as the 'me decade' because of the preoccupation with 'my needs' and 'let's talk about me' approaches.

All this undoubtedly indicated a deep spiritual hunger. It was illustrated by one of my colleagues who described his own pilgrimage from 'rational humanism' to 'devotional humanism', by which he meant a discovery of a need for meditation and personal values based upon what now would be called 'green issues'. Words such as 'fulfilment', 'wholeness' and 'integration', often described in almost spiritual terms, began to appear in psychiatric texts, although any attempt to see these as deriving from a religious or theistic context was met with a sharp rebuttal.

This development, coupled with pluralism with its many philosophical positions and religious beliefs, has led to psychiatrists becoming increasingly aware that they can no longer ignore the belief structures and the value systems of their patients. Their attitude became that either these are cultural variants and 'true' and valid for the individuals concerned but requiring no response from scientific psychiatry, or, as one leading psychiatrist expressed in a paper to the Royal Society of Health, 'There is a significant element in life and health to do with meaning, which is concerned with the direction of one's life . . . the psychiatrist should allow the patient to develop and express his own spiritual values. . . .' He went on to suggest that one of the functions of the psychiatrist may be 'helping the patient to find his god'.[1]

The fact that antidepressants and other psychotropic medication have been so successful in treating the more severe psychiatric disorders has led to increasing attention being directed to lesser disorders. An example of this is the anxiety and depression which often occur in family relationships. In the 1950s, marital problems and their associated distress would have been dismissed by many psychiatrists as inappropriate referrals to a psychiatric clinic. By the 1970s, marital problems and marital therapy merited a whole section in a postgraduate text on 'Recent Advances in Psychiatry', where it was argued that it was 'better to encourage the breakup of a relationship which was unfulfilling for one or other party where there was the possibility of forming a more fulfilling relationship subsequently'.[2] This was in spite of the fact that the author acknowledged that there were no scientific or follow-up studies available to support his suggestion and that second marriages have a higher rate of breakdown than first ones. At the time, it was received wisdom that children would be happier to be removed from a situation where their parents were constantly bickering or in conflict. My own reflection was that children more often wished their parents to remain together, and, if forced to make such a choice, were influenced more by where security seemed to lie; where teddy bear was tended to be more influential than which parent to select. This was quite apart from the observation that every broken relationship makes it more difficult to believe in the permanence of any subsequent relationship. It was the pioneering and persistent work of a practising Christian, Dr Jack Dominian, who patiently conducted studies in his Family Research Unit in London, which confirmed the high degree of mental and physical illness arising out of divorce and family breakup, quite apart from the enormous cost to the nation economically.

These issues have rightly gained the attention of the press and have resulted in much closer scrutiny of the assumption that *desires* are the same as *rights*, and one's own fulfilment is good. A *Times* leader (21 May 1990) commented:

> The 1960s consensus that quick and easy divorce was in the best interests of all parties is increasingly open to doubt. Experts now say that we have underestimated the damage done to children by divorce. Moreover a surprising number of people who get divorced then regret it. The problem seems to be that once an unhappy couple approach a lawyer they are driven to divorce as inexorably as the military mobilisations in the summer of 1914 led to war.

It has to be said that many psychiatrists and social scientists were not far behind the alleged activity of the lawyers in the pressure put upon individuals, even within a so-called therapeutic situation. Even if there was no attempt to impose values and beliefs upon patients or to bring emotional pressure to bear upon individuals in a time of great vulnerability, I often felt that there was less than honest dealing with such individuals when the specialists too readily accepted the value system of the patient under treatment.

The psalmist in Psalm 8:4 asked the question 'What is man?', and the writer of Ecclesiastes debated with himself regarding the meaning of life. The lusty Roman poet Ovid, with no background of Jewish thought or contact, nevertheless echoed the words of St Paul in Romans 7 when he said, 'I see the better things and I agree with them, but I follow the worse.' Such questions are asked as often today as in former days; one leading psychiatrist identifies this as 'man is still searching for a map of man'. His own solution was that provided by traditional psychoanalysis. In this century the emergence of biological and behavioural sciences has produced several 'maps of man', from psycho-analysis to behaviour modification, in an attempt to under-stand man and thereby to heal or resolve his tensions. One researcher on human sexuality summed up his conclusions after decades of study and research in the following words:

> Paradoxically further study of the continually increasing volume of publications has led to less firm opinions than before. Increas-ing awareness of the complexities of the subject brings with it the realisation that on many issues it would be wise to suspend judg-ment pending further research. Indeed one conclusion that can be expressed without fear of contradiction is that much more needs to be learnt about human sexuality even before quite elementary questions can be answered with any degree of confidence.[3]

Experience suggests that further research could make him even less sure.

One of the prerequisites of the 'ideal psychiatrist' is 'the ability to be detached at times from any value judgment', able to be 'accepting and totally free of prejudice (an ability only found in those who genuinely possess very well defined values and have a personality that is mature).'[4] It is an error to believe that only those without well defined, and hopefully thought out values are tolerant and accept-ing. On the contrary, the absence of such values and beliefs may be dangerous.

Dualism

Harry Williams, writing of his experience as a psychiatric patient stated:

A psychiatrist should be chosen because he is a skilled psychiatrist and not because he is a good Catholic or reads the Bible every morning. I have a lasting suspicion of people who are known as a *Christian* dentist or a *Christian* doctor or a *Christian* psychiatrist or a *Christian* chiropodist. Invariably it means that they are bad at their craft. God is honoured by a dentist being a good dentist, not by his singing hymns.[5]

He rightly points to the fear of psychiatrists in the minds of many Christians who protect themselves and their beliefs by insisting on a 'Christian psychiatrist'. I agree entirely with this and strongly believe that the prerequisite of a good psychiatrist is that he should be someone respected as a person of ability, integrity and of good standing among his colleagues, including non-psychiatrists. I do not believe that it necessarily helps for the worldview of the patient to be understood by the psychiatrist; what is important is the open acknowledgement and discussion of where worldviews differ and an acceptance by both psychiatrist and patient as to the limits upon such issues. Openness and honesty is often all that is necessary in order to establish a good therapeutic relationship between doctor and patient, even when worldviews and value systems are disparate.

However, the philosophical and antireligious bias of Freud, especially as portrayed by some of his followers, has led to the public perception of psychiatrists as generally being anti-God and hostile to Christian belief, even though Freud's views have not been a dominant influence upon the practice of psychiatry in this country. Few psychiatrists in Britain hold the rigid philosophical and reductionist views of men like Maudsley, Freud and Sargant, and they would be unhappy to stray far from such a position in their practice. This has had a generally beneficial result in ensuring a pragmatic approach to the severer forms of psychiatric illness, ensuring treatment with proven and scientifically assessed methods of treatment.

The same has not been so true when psychiatrists have

dealt with patients with lesser forms of psychiatric disorder, with some of the results mentioned previously. This has led to a fear of the practice of psychiatry in many Christian medical students and young doctors; although they are attracted to dealing with patients on a broader basis than purely the physical, they are unhappy with the reputed hostility of psychiatrists to religious faith. They are often confirmed in this view by senior doctors, not least those known for a Christian commitment but sceptical about the value of psychiatry, largely out of deficiencies in their own training. Such individuals often profess to be fearful for the continued spiritual wellbeing of any Christian who should enter into the practice of such a subject. I personally am grateful to the canny Scots physician who quietly encouraged me in my medical student days, on the ground that 'There is a need for Christians to practise psychiatry and demonstrate that it is possible to be truly scientific in one's thinking and at the same time committed to Christ'.

A small pamphlet which I wrote, called *Starting Psychiatry*, was published to help Christian medical students embarking on their psychiatric studies and experiencing difficulties with the special problems posed by the nature of the suffering of these patients and special language and approaches of psychiatry.[6] It is a booklet which has remained in print for twenty years and has, I hope, contributed something to the changed attitudes which have resulted in many more Christian doctors being prepared to pursue a career in psychiatry than twenty years ago.

In it I focused upon the need for Christian and non-Christian alike to examine their attitudes, lest they be guilty of smuggling their own special prejudices and preconceptions into their practice of medicine. Such self-examination is not easy, as it means calling into question one's own beliefs, standards and objectives in life when faced with patients and colleagues who would hold very different views on life and may have quite deliberately and specifically rejected a Christian standpoint.

Unfortunately, there is still a strongly held view among both Christians and non-Christians that mental illness is something to be ashamed of, and that it is self-induced. The approach to the mentally ill adopted by such individuals is to search for some approach, often a panacea, along the lines that if only one's diet, exercise, lifestyle or some procedure is rigorously held to, then all mental disorder will disappear. In some Christian circles, conversion, or special healing procedures, or exorcism would be spiritual counterparts. These, of course, are no different from the 'nothing but' approaches so frequently encountered in the philosophical framework of the materialist and atheist, and are equally reductionist. The temptation to resort to quick solutions is always present. Anything which appears to offer *solutions* and *cure* is always more seductive and attractive than the preparedness to accept that in human behaviour and illness, *resolution* and *relief* is more usual. Inexperience and lack of familiarity with patients often leads the medical student and young psychiatrist to become impatient with a person who 'won't be cured', and to take a punitive approach to them. Among Christians there is the often-expressed belief that 'if only' a patient would become a Christian then all difficulties would disappear. In fact, quite the reverse may occur. Becoming a Christian may produce extra conflict in a person who finds himself at greater variance with his family and with colleagues as he faces challenges to an established lifestyle.

Often there is a dualism in Christian thinking which reduces everything in life to either the organic or the spiritual, and refuses to look at research which demonstrates that our experiences and mental processes are a complex interaction of the effects of our genetic background, family and upbringing, life events, and goals in life. Some Christians are reluctant to look at the very human issues behind their illness and instead demand 'spiritual remedies' from the Christian psychiatrist, having already exhausted their normal spiritual mentors. The plethora of 'how to overcome ...' books in secular bookshops have their parallel in Christian books supporting a thriving Christian alternative medicine, avidly backed by those keen to have a personalised medicine but not prepared to subject the claims of such 'Christian therapies' to proper evaluation.[7]

Conclusion

Psychiatrists are faced with many who have lived their life in such a way that pain, grief and depression have been the almost inevitable fruit of their conduct, and others who have had unfulfilled goals and objectives in their work and relationships. The psychiatrist has to explore the roots of his patient's behaviour, help him retrace his steps and find a new purpose for going forward in life. Whatever happens, no psychiatrist should force his own belief or faith upon a patient. Such an act would be a fundamental transgression of the professional nature of the doctor/patient relationship which can never be an equal relationship, and even less so where the patient's judgement may be impaired and vulnerability increased by psychiatric illness. Sadly, many Christians have felt that their problems have been blamed entirely upon their Christian viewpoint, but it also has to be said that many Christian patients have refused to examine how little thought-through and reality-based their own faith has been. As a result, they have criticised unjustly their psychiatrist, be he non-Christian or Christian, for seeking to explore discrepancies in their own belief and behaviour.

Perhaps the reason why the medical profession has a significantly higher incidence of alcohol abuse and suicide than many professions derives from the fact that such issues are seldom raised in the training of medical students or postgraduates. Trying to deal with patients who have presented with deliberate self-harm, diseases incurred by abuse, in addition to those who have suffered from the malevolence of fate or even members of their own family, brings distress and even despair which cannot always be assuaged by more research, more precise definitions or increased devotion to one's work.

The theologian, J.I. Packer, has said, 'Man is a biologically developed, language-using, tool-making, social, economic, political animal with a complicated physiology and even more complicated psychology . . . and that is to say nothing about the historical and philosophical contributions to our understanding of man.' That does not mean that we ought to interpret biblical language as equivalent to any behavioural jargon in vogue; this would reduce ultimate truth to dependence on a limited culture-dependent understanding of man. It does not mean that we should read Freudian concepts into biblical terminology, equating the ego with the soul and the superego with conscience. It does not mean that we should use biblical terminology and words as though Scripture had to include some allusion to every possible discovery of man, or that the Bible is a mini-treatise in psychology or behavioural sciences. It does mean that we have to use the insights of all that science and research have made available in the realm of human experience and conflict, while remaining sceptical as to these being the last word.

As a psychiatrist I have to deal with the lives of men and women in illness, conflict and tension. But I myself need to be wrestling at the same time with the biblical revelation regarding the human condition and man's ultimate need. The first illumines the second, but the second gives the context within which the first is to be understood and explored. Here is the framework within which I approach my patients and assess the current practice of psychiatry, aware that there is no easy synthesis but an ongoing fight against a blinkered scientism on the one hand and an easy believism on the other. Even 'good doctors' can slip into either error.

At the end of the day, the psychiatrist who is a Christian knows the limitations of his work. He knows that new discoveries will be made about God's creation and about human behaviour. But he also believes that something new happened when God the Creator of all came to live among men in the Person of Jesus, that he died on a cross for us and rose again from the dead to bring new life to all who put their trust in him. This is at the heart of my life.

As a psychiatrist, I am tempted to agree with the writer of Ecclesiastes who said that there was nothing new on the face of the earth. Finding a meaning in life and a god who suits undoubtedly helps people, but it is possible to miss or refuse to meet the only God who is the basis of all life. I cannot give a meaning for life to be dispensed like pills and therapy; I can receive the confessions of wrongs and listen to the outpourings of guilt so that people feel better, but only Jesus Christ can forgive and remove guilt. As a psychiatrist I can encourage, challenge and direct people to act differently, but only the Spirit of God ultimately gives people new power to act as God wills; I can explore possibilities and ways of living a better and different life, but Jesus Christ is the only Person who has said, 'I *am* the way, the truth and the life, no one comes to the Father except through me' (Jn 14:6). These are strong words which draw their credibility from the life, teaching, death and resurrection of Jesus Christ, and it is to him that I seek to witness as a Christian.

Notes

[1] A.C.P. Sims, 'The Psychiatrist as a Priest', *Hospital Update* (November 1988), p 2129.

[2] S. Crown, *Recent Advances in Psychiatry* (Duckworth, 1971), p 201.

[3] D.J. West, *Homosexuality Re-examined* (Duckworth, 1977), p 316.

[4] K. Jaspers, *General Psychopathology* (Manchester University Press, 1963), pp 808–809.

[5] H. Williams, *Someday I'll Find You* (Mitchell Beazley, 1982), p 167.
[6] M.G. Barker, *Starting Psychiatry* (CMF, 1971).
[7] These are issues explored further in two papers by the author: 'Biblical and Psychological Methods of Pastoral Care' in Malcolm Jeeves (ed), *Behavioural Sciences: a Christian Perspective* (IVP, 1984), pp 230–245; 'Psychological Aspects of Inner Healing' in Nigel Cameron and Sinclair Ferguson (eds), *Pulpit and People* (Rutherford House: Edinburgh, 1986), pp 89–102.

14

To Whale or not to Whale, That is the Question

Ray Gambell – Conservation biologist

Dr Ray Gambell, BSc, PhD.
Born 1935. Educated Kingsbury County School and Reading University.
Whale Research Unit, Institute of Oceanographic Sciences, 1963–76.
Scientific adviser to UK delegation of International Whaling Commission, 1965–76.
Secretary, International Whaling Commission since 1976.

'You seem a nice enough bloke; what are you doing in this bloody whaling business?' The Australian TV interviewer had hoped to catch me off guard, jet-lagged and tired after flying from London to Sydney. He had reduced his Prime Minister to tears in a recent broadcast, and had a reputation as a tough interviewer to maintain. What was I, what am I, doing in the whaling business?

My involvement had started in a normal enough way. After graduating in zoology, I thought it important as a Christian to do something 'useful' with my biological training. I had made my commitment and become a Christian in my second term as a student, so growth in the Christian life and scientific training had proceeded together. I began in fisheries research, and although counting whiting vertebrae may not be an immediately obvious way to provide food for a hungry world, it was one contribution to the knowledge necessary to identify the stocks of a renewable resource so that they can be properly managed and harvested on a sustainable basis. Together with age determination, maturity rates, recruitment and the rest of their vital parameters, the lives of the fish are reduced to components in an equation leading to catch limits, the mesh sizes of the fishermen's nets and the rest of the regulatory measures needed to prevent over-fishing.

In the early 1960s, the international regulation of whaling was at a crisis point, with obvious depletion of the major stocks of these largest of the mammals, but little quantitative science to provide the factual basis for rational management. I was fortunate then to have the chance to move on from fish to bigger things and so became a whale biologist, and later the scientific advisor on whales to the UK government, and subsequently an international administrator.

Scientific research

The scientific ethic, indeed the attitude of research scientists in general, is one of intellectual honesty in a genuine seeking after the truth. This is totally compatible with the Christian view of life and work; being both a scientist and a Christian does not introduce any special strains in integrity when dealing with fellow scientists, or anyone else for that matter. But that does not mean that there are not temptations comparable with those we may experience in other walks of life.

By its very nature, a great deal of scientific research consists of repetitive and unexciting work. There is an increasing requirement for results which will stand up to rigorous statistical analysis. This calls for large numbers of observations to be collected, measurements made or samples examined to build up a data base which will provide unequivocal answers with computed means and standard errors. But biological systems do not always conform to the expected patterns which the researchers put forward as the hypothesis to be tested in their experimental design. Thus there may be a temptation to leave out the odd aberrant record which falls far off the nicely constructed line on the graph. The picture would look so much prettier if the wayward measurement was not there, the statistical variance would be reduced and the whole thing would be far more conclusive.

This is a temptation which must come to all research scientists at one time or another. There are some classic cases of apparently 'constructed' results in scientific papers which could not have been achieved by the professed experimental techniques used. But the honest approach, and certainly one which a Christian must adopt, is to record and report things as they are and not as we may like them to be, however inconvenient that might prove. The biblical injunction on this matter is very clear: 'Do not lie to one another' (Col 3:9).

The problem becomes more acute when the results produced by the scientist are applied in some practical way by third parties, such as administrators or legislators, who do not have the background to assess the validity of the recommendations or the guidance offered.

A particular case in the whaling context bears on this kind of situation.

The age of whales

In many management procedures for living resources it is important to know the age structure for the population under consideration. However, measuring the age of whales was a problem for a long time in the history of modern whale research. A number of different techniques were tried, various tissues of the body were investigated, but with rather little success. Then, in 1955, work carried out in the British Museum (Natural History) on the hearing mechanism of whales showed that the earplug of the fin whale is made up of a series of alternating lighter and darker growth layers which might be used as a basis for age determination. It was quickly shown that by counting these growth layers, the age of the whale can be determined in the same way as the rings in a tree trunk indicate its age.

At the time of this breakthrough there appeared to be good reasons, derived from migratory behaviour and other evidence, for believing that the growth layers are formed at the rate of two pairs of alternating light and dark zones per year. On this timescale the scientists had advised their government representatives at the International Whaling Commission to reduce the permitted catches to certain levels in order that the stocks should not be further depleted.

The Antarctic whale fishery was verging on economic extinction in 1964, and the Commission itself was on the point of collapse through the inability of the member governments to reach agreement on how to conserve the whale stocks. Surprisingly in these circumstances, the Commission agreed to reduce the Antarctic catch limits over the next three years to below the sustainable yields of the stocks as estimated by the best scientific advice available. It was therefore a severe blow to realise that we scientists had got the age determination wrong, that only one pair of light and dark growth zones are laid down each year. Thus the whales actually live for twice as long as we first thought, but reproduce at half the rate previously used to determine the catch limits. After having reached such a hard-fought agreement to reduce the catches to certain levels, it was particularly difficult in the face of political pressure and representations from the industry to say that the catches needed to be reduced to something like a half of what was expected on the basis of the earlier scientific advice. But that was what had to be done to be truthful and honest to the facts.

Political pressures

Whaling is a highly emotive subject, and, until recent years at least, has been a main target for the international conservation community. Ever since the 1972 United Nations Conference on the Human Environment, held in Stockholm, 'Save the Whale' has been the rallying cry in these circles. Extreme views have been expressed and violent and sometimes criminal actions have been adopted in attempts to change the inherently conservative positions of the governments and authorities maintaining the industry. My policy has always been to be as evenhanded and objective as possible in the face of whatever provocation might come. Certainly, it has been important to be known as someone whose 'yea is yea' (Jas 5:12), for any appearance of partiality would lose the credibility necessary for the diplomatic and political negotiations involved.

We have had to evacuate a meeting while the bomb squad dealt with a suspicious packet, I and others have been moved from one hotel to another under assumed names by the police to avoid trouble, and in the worst incident the Japanese delegates were attacked and had red ink thrown over them by demonstrators who broke into the annual diplomatic conference of the IWC. From my own experience, it is not at all comfortable to be approached by someone from the crowd at a press conference who throws liquid at your face because you are doing a job with which he disagrees. Fortunately for me it was not acid but tomato ketchup, but the psychological shock and trauma are as great.

In all these situations it is necessary to be sure of your own position, to be certain that what you are doing is right before God, and to be ready to deal with the events of the moment in that light.

Other pressures

The economics of the whaling industry and the passions of those opposed to whaling can result in situations where inducements are offered for certain actions to be taken which might not otherwise occur, just as businessmen offer hospitality to their customers or other influential people.

At one time during the late 1970s, the IWC had a ban which was flouted by a whaling operation sailing under a succession of 'flags of convenience'. The purpose was simply to get round the agreed restrictions designed to conserve the whale stocks, and there seemed to be rather little that could be done under international law to prevent the abuse. However, when the IWC decided that its member governments should not import the products of whaling originating from non-IWC sources, this effectively closed the market for this 'pirate' operation. The owner of the whaling fleet was very concerned, for he had a considerable quantity of whale meat stored in deep freeze which he could no longer sell. He came to me as Secretary of the IWC to try to get some kind of accommodation in the matter. Any action which allowed the meat to enter into international trade was obviously contrary to IWC policy, but he did offer half the value of the meat (£500,000) as an inducement which could have been used for research or any other purpose. This offer was not really tempting, for the Christian knows that 'You shall take no bribe, for a bribe blinds the officials, and subverts the cause of those who are in the right' (Ex 23:8). It is easy to see, though, how people can so easily get into unfortunate tangles when the end seems to justify the means.

There have also been pressures from the other side of the whale war. At a particularly difficult public meeting I was howled down on the platform as I attempted to explain the work done by the IWC. The audience, or some members of it, were not prepared to listen to any arguments except their own, and were determined to prevent any other view being expressed. The organisers of the meeting managed to restore some kind of order in the end so that I could complete my presentation, and then took me out for a meal afterwards. It was clear that they were embarrassed by what had taken place, and yet at the same time they had a good deal of sympathy with the vocal members of the audience and wished to influence me towards that point of view. By the end of the evening it was made very clear as we walked back to the hotel that I was welcome to return home with one of the young ladies of the group.

The expectation that influence might be applied and used in particular ways can come from any direction. There are a number of people involved in the whaling issue who think that their ends may be attained by applying pressure or providing favours. It is indeed disturbing to find that some of them are not above using knowingly false information to advance the cause which they hold so passionately. The evidence which has been presented by certain anti-whaling advocates to some congressional committees of the United States Government has been flagrantly distorted and untrue. To them, the end of whaling must be such an important goal to achieve that any means, fair or foul, is legitimate. However, the Bible makes it plain in a number of places that we should always 'Speak the truth to one another' (Zech 8:16), and 'Putting away falsehood, let every one speak the truth with his neighbour' (Eph 4:25).

Conclusion

So what am I doing in the whaling business? Whales are fascinating creatures with many features in their biology, physiology and behaviour which make them particularly interesting subjects to study. Their bodies also represent a significant source of food and other raw materials. These sometimes conflicting aspects highlight a number of the problems we have to face in the world with respect to our role as stewards of God's creation.

Our care of the natural world, or lack of care, which has resulted in overexploitation of a number of species, including the whales, is clearly of concern to many people, not just Christians. It is important therefore to see that the world's wealth is not wasted, or used in trivial ways, but made available for all mankind including future generations. That is consistent with God's command to love our neighbours (Mt 22:39). It seems important to me to be involved in the processes which decide on our use and treatment of whales, whether they should be hunted at all, and if they are, with such matters as the humaneness of the killing process, as well as the setting of safe catch limits. So for me this has included basic research into the lives of whales, and more recently, involvement in the politics and decision-making processes of governments.

Because the Christian believes that God created the world in which we live and that he has given us responsibility for its care, we have a special cause for glorifying in his handiwork and marvelling at the complexity and beauty of the creation. But this also means that we do not see the exploitation of the world's resources, whether well regulated or not, as the only point of life. Rather, we see such utilisation in the broader context of the whole of God's dealings with us, our own relationships with one another, and with God. In one way this makes our care of the earth all the more important; in another, it places it at a rather different level, for 'Great are the works of the Lord, studied by all who have pleasure in them' (Ps 111:2).

15

Genes, Genesis and Greens

Sam Berry – Evolutionary biologist

Professor R.J. (Sam) Berry, MA, PhD, DSc, F I Biol, FRSE.
Born 1934. Educated Kirkham Grammar School, Shrewsbury School, Gonville and Caius College, Cambridge, and University College, London.
Professor of Genetics in the University of London since 1974.
Member, Natural Environment Research Council, 1981–87.
President, Linnean Society, 1982–85.
President, British Ecological Society, 1987–89.
President European Ecological Federation, 1990–92.
Vice-President, Zoological Society of London, 1988–1990.
Chairman, Research Scientists' Christian Fellowship (now Christians in Science), 1968–88.
Member, General Synod of the Church of England, 1970–90.
Trustee, National Museums and Galleries on Merseyside from 1986.
Governor, Monkton Combe School, Bath, from 1979.

My father committed suicide when I was in the sixth form at school, working for A levels. I had been sent to boarding school because my mother was incapacitated with multiple sclerosis. As an only child, my father had thought it better for me to be away from home.

Because of my mother's illness, my father and I were particularly close, and his action was proportionately more difficult for me to understand. My memory is of coming home for the inquest and funeral, and going for long walks by myself, asking why? why? why? I don't know if I was a real Christian at that time. When I joined the Boy Scouts, I had been told that I ought to go to church because my Scout's promise included a commitment to 'honour God'. I used to haul my father along on most Sundays to a dreary and incomprehensible ritual at our local parish church. I took my confirmation (at boarding school) seriously, and later learned that the school chaplain had preached the Sunday before the confirmation service on the text 'Behold, I [Jesus] stand at the door and knock; if any man hear my voice, and open the door, I will come in' (Rev 3:20). I remember the occasion, and know that I followed the steps in his exposition. But three years later, I could discern no meaning in life nor understand why my father decided 'to take his life while the balance of his mind was temporarily disturbed'.

The summer after my father's death I went to a house-party run by the Scripture Union. There I heard that the death of Jesus Christ at Calvary was not simply the end of an inspired teacher or the defeat of a promising liberation movement, but was God's intervention to provide a way back into his purpose for all who accepted him at his word, including me. In hackneyed words, 'everything fell into place'. The explanation of the New Testament events was intellectually satisfying and blindingly obvious. Like Thomas Henry Huxley a century earlier, who commented on reading Darwin's *Origin of Species,* 'how stupid not to have thought of that oneself', I was rationally convinced of what I later discovered was the Christian gospel of 'salvation through grace alone'.

My acceptance of Christ as my Saviour is relevant because it was to me at the time (indeed, looking back, ever since that August day in 1952) a completely logical response to a reasoned argument on a par with the rigour expected in my A level science studies. I had planned to be a doctor and had already a provisional offer of a place in the medical school at Cambridge. A few months later, I realised that I would not be happy spending my life coping with other people at first hand, and, in the first event which, in retrospect, showed me God's nudging Spirit, I changed from a medical to a biology course.

As a Christian at university, I was faced with a hierarchy of possibilities. The really holy people became missionaries, the rather holy people were ordained, and the fairly holy people became teachers; the 'also rans' did all the other jobs in the world. I hope I was prepared to serve abroad if God wanted me there, but I felt no particular call. I was tempted to train for the Church of England ministry, but two weeks of 'testing my vocation' proved to me that God did not want me in that job; just as I would have been a terrible doctor, I would also have been a disastrous parson. So I started applying for school teaching posts—but no one offered me a job. I assumed God had a purpose for my life, but it wasn't very clear. The line of least resistance was to do the minimum; I stayed in the university world, working for a PhD in genetics at University College, London. And, despite having pushed a few doors, I have remained in the university world; since 1974, I have been Professor of Genetics in the University of London.

Linked to the false assumption about the sanctity of various jobs that was around in my Cambridge days was a parallel belief that all Christians were supposed to be evangelists. My problem was that I had none of the gifts possessed by some of getting alongside people and proclaiming Christ. It was a great relief when I realised that we have all been given different talents and callings, and that there is not (and should not) be such a thing as a typical or normal Christian. This is not an excuse to avoid living and speaking for Christ at every appropriate opportunity; rather, it is a recognition that 'the chief end of man is to glorify

God and to enjoy him for ever' (as defined in the *Westminster Catechism*), which does not necessarily mean that we are supposed primarily to operate as more or less full-time evangelists.

Looking back, it took me some time to accept that I was in a place that God had prepared for me. After all, making microscopical preparations of mouse embryos (which was the main practical work in my PhD studies), or catching radioactive rats in India, or melanic moths in Shetland, or limpets in the Antarctic, are not usually considered to be spiritual activities. But, like a number of other contributors in this volume, I have no doubts that God has wanted me as a scientist, and that he has given me work to do for him because I was in the place he had prepared for me.

Evolutionary biology

When I first began to learn biology at school, it appeared to be a hotchpotch of facts and ideas—interesting but disconnected. Only when we were introduced to evolution did everything start to make sense; it became possible to recognise patterns in classification, distribution, development and biological history. It was the same at university. By then I was vaguely aware of the nineteenth-century debates about Genesis and evolution, but they remained shadowy until a medical student friend whom I had taken to hear a number of evangelistic sermons informed me that it would be intellectually dishonest for him to become a Christian because he 'would not be allowed to believe in evolution'. Of course I told him that was nonsense, that neither belief nor disbelief in evolution had anything to do with his relationship with the crucified Christ, but he would not be swayed.

I do not doubt that my friend's views about evolution were an excuse to avoid commitment—although they were real to him at the time. But they made me go back both to the Bible creation stories and to the history of the evolution-creation controversy. It rapidly became clear to me that much of the argument was about interpretation rather than basic doctrine. The Genesis account of creation is of a progress from nothing (or more accurately, God only) through geological and biological change to mankind. Nowhere in the Bible are we told the mechanisms God used to carry out his work; indeed, we only know by faith that God is involved (Heb 11:3). The normal Hebrew term used for God's creating activity in Genesis is *asah*, which is the word for shaping existing material, like a potter moulding clay. Another word (*bara*) is used for God's creation of matter, life and mankind, implying a different and specifically divine act. This should not be taken to mean that God necessarily made our body from scratch, as it were; we are distinguished from the rest of creation by God's image in us (Gen 1:26–27), not genetically or anatomically. In other words, there is no biblical reason why we should not be descended from animal ancestors; the important element is that we are subject and responsible to God in a qualitatively different way to the rest of creation.

There are, of course, other superficial conflicts between the scientific understanding of evolution and the biblical record, but none are serious. For example, the 'day' framework of creation in Genesis 1 can be interpreted in a number of ways other than as a series of literal twenty-four-hour periods. Indeed, the statement that 'God rested' on the seventh day (Ex 20:11) cannot be taken literally, because our God never sleeps (Ps 121:4); this suggests that the week of creation should not be regarded as a calendar week; but it does indicate that one of the many lessons we can learn from God's establishment of the natural order is the importance of a regular rhythm of work and rest.

As a professional scientist, I am often asked to speak about my faith to Christian groups. At a meeting for Christian doctors in Australia (whither I had gone to trap mice on the sub-Antarctic Macquarie Island), I was urged to write down my understanding of the creation events, because it seemed both scriptural and helpful to that audience of educated men and women. This led to a book first published as *Adam and the Ape* in 1975, and revised as *God and Evolution* in 1988. I often meet people who thank me for publishing my ideas, since they are more convincing to them than the traditional understanding of God as the Great Watchmaker who made the world in a 6-day period 6,000 years ago. I frequently wonder why the old view persists as stubbornly as it does. My provisional belief is that 'creationists'[1] are frightened of the challenge of a God who is Lord of change as well as of changelessness, and who may surprise by his demands and unexpectedness; in other words, 'creationism' can be a wall against God himself. The irony is that Charles Darwin destroyed the intellectual legitimacy of a God who is separated from his world, and forced us to recognise that he is also present in processes and mechanisms. In theological language, God is both transcendent and immanent.

Miracles

At the same time that I was working out the positive lessons to be drawn from the evolution–creation controversy, I was moving in my research from developmental to ecological genetics (I wanted to study how developmental processes influenced population processes), which in effect means the study of evolutionary mechanisms operating in living populations. In other words, I became an evolutionary biologist. I acquired various responsibilities outside my university duties. From 1982 to 1985 I was President of the Linnean Society, the oldest biological society in the world, and the one to which the original papers of Darwin and Wallace on evolution by natural selection were read in 1858. I was aware of how careful I had to be. Thomas Bell, who was President of the Society in 1858, summed up at the end of the year, it 'has not been marked by any of the striking discoveries which revolutionise the department of science on which they bear. . . .' I will not comment!

Involvement at the national level widens one's horizons and makes one aware of the responsibilities and opportunities to attempt positive contributions. In 1984, there was a debate in Britain about the beliefs of church leaders, and in particular whether miracles are still credible in a 'scientific age'. It seemed right to criticise the sloppy thinking being bandied about, and I co-ordinated a letter to the London *Times* about miracles. Fourteen of us signed the letter; all of us were professors of science. We asserted:

> It is not logically valid to use science as an argument against miracles. To believe that miracles cannot happen is as much an act of faith as to believe that they can happen. We gladly accept the virgin birth, the Gospel miracles, and the resurrection of Christ as historical events. . . . Miracles are unprecedented events. Whatever the current fashion in philosophy or the revelations of opinion polls may suggest, it is important to affirm that science (based as it is upon the observation of precedents) can have nothing to say on the subject. Its 'laws' are only generalizations of our experience... (*The Times*, 13 July 1984).

The following week, a leading article in the scientific journal *Nature* appeared, agreeing with our statement on the nature of scientific laws, but dissenting from our conclusion about miracles, calling them

> inexplicable and irreproducible phenomena [which] do not occur—a definition by exclusion of the concept . . . the publication of Berry *et al* provides a licence not merely for religious belief (which on other grounds is unexceptionable), but for mischievous reports of all things paranormal, from ghosts to flying saucers.

The editor of *Nature* received a number of letters dissenting from his argument, and, to his credit, he published them. One correspondent objected that 'your concern not to license "mischievous reports of all things paranormal" is no doubt motivated in the interest of scientific truth, but your strategy of defining away what you find unpalatable is the antithesis of scientific'.[2] A letter from Donald MacKay in the same issue emphasised that

for the Christian believer, baseless credulity is a sin—a disservice to the God of truth. His belief in the resurrection does not stem from softness in his standards of evidence, but rather from the coherence with which (as he sees it) that particular unprecedented event fits into and makes sense of a great mass of data. . . . There is clearly no inconsistency in believing (with astonishment) in a unique event so well attested, while remaining unconvinced by spectacular stories of 'paranormal' occurrences that lack any comparable support.

I was then invited to reply to the correspondence; my response was published in *Nature* in 1986.[3] I concluded my article,

The conventional view of miracles is that they depend on supernatural intervention in, or suspension of, the natural order. Some theologians have been over-impressed with scientific determinism, and have attempted a demythologized (miracle-free) religion. This endeavour is now unfashionable, but it is worse than that; Nebelsick (a Scottish theologian) called it 'a speculative device imposed on unsuspecting persons . . . based on false presuppositions about both science and the scientific world view'. This is no help to scientists, and an interventionist God will always be an embarrassment to us.

I believe the interpretation that miracles are a necessary but unpredictable consequence of a God who holds the world in being is more plausible and more scriptural than deist interventionism (ie, the nineteenth-century distortion of the doctrine of God, who was assumed to be nothing more than a Divine Watchmaker). This does not mean that apparent miracles should be approached with any less objectivity than we would employ for any scientific observation; our standards of evidence should be just as rigorous. Those who deny the possibility of miracles are exercising their own brand of faith; this is based on a questionable assumption, and one which creates problems with its implications. Miracles in the New Testament are described as unusual events which are wonders due to God's power, intended as signs. Confining oneself wholly to this category (leaving aside the question of whether other sorts of miracles occur), this makes at least some miracles acceptable and non-capricious, and independent of our knowledge of their mechanism.

The appearance of a long article on miracles in a journal such as *Nature* inevitably caused a stir. The President of the American Statistical Association devoted his presidential address to a discussion of the implication of miracles for probability theory.[4] It produced some adverse reaction. But it established clearly that we have a rationally defensible faith. Obviously not everyone will agree with our interpretation, but a faith based on the Scriptures cannot be dismissed as woolly wishful thinking. Like the psalmist, in words carved on the doors of the old Cavendish Laboratory in Cambridge (where Lord Rutherford directed much of the early research on atomic structure), we can affirm 'Great are the works of the Lord, studied by all who have pleasure therein' (Ps 111:2).

Conservation and stewardship

One of the sadnesses of the evolution–creation debate is that it has delayed the proper understanding of God's trusting his creation to us. Christians have been so busy defending their personal interpretation of Scripture that they have neglected to work out the implications of the creation narratives. As we approach the end of the twentieth century and face increasing problems with pollution, over-population, poverty, and climate change, we are having to define a proper attitude to nature. This is a problem for everyone, but Christians have a special responsibility if they believe in a creating and sustaining God who holds mankind accountable for the gifts and privileges given to them.

In 1980, the International Union for the Conservation of Nature and the United Nations Environmental Programme issued a World Conservation Strategy (WCS), arguing that we misuse the resources of the planet to our own detriment. Good environmental behaviour was, according to the WCS, simply self-interest.

All member nations of the United Nations Environmental Programme were required to respond to the WCS. The United Kingdom's response was in several parts (urban, rural, industrial, etc) and included an ethics section, which I was asked to write. I pointed out a deficiency in the WCS: our attitude to the environment is determined by four valuations—to ourselves, our community, future generations, and nature itself; from the secular point of view the first three can be justified on utilitarian grounds, but nature's own interest is understandable from this standpoint only if we identify ourselves as inseparable from nature. This option is the route taken by the 'deep greens' and by the New Age (the two are not necessarily the same). However, to a Christian, nature is valuable because it is God's—created by him and declared to be good. A scriptural view thus gives weight to all four interests, and should be proclaimed positively by all Christians.

Unfortunately, Christians are often attacked on the grounds that the Bible is said to teach that man has an obligation to use the world's resources for himself ('have dominion' as a ruler), and to reproduce unrestrainably (Gen 1:28). Both assumptions are wrong. God's command to 'have dominion' is given explicitly to mankind made in God's image. His concern is that we are responsible to him for his world; in other words, we are stewards of the world's resources, answerable to God as the owner (see Lk 12:13–48; 19:12–27; 20:9–18). And family size is a part of our responsibility; the command to reproduce applied to the chosen people of the Old Testament, but physical continuity was replaced by spiritual spread in Christ's regime. The creation ordinance to 'fill the earth' with our physical children should now be interpreted as an obligation to spread Christ's rule on earth 'by making disciples of every nation' (Mt 28:19–20). (The idea that contraception is 'unnatural' is based on the notion that God works through largely immutable laws; it diminishes in importance once we accept that God is active—and sovereign—in natural processes.)

My involvement with the World Conservation Strategy had a sequel when, in 1989, I was asked to help prepare a Code of Environmental Practice for the Economic Summit Nations (Canada, France, Germany, Italy, Japan, Britain and the United States). The Code we produced was based on an environmental ethic, involving 'Stewardship of the living and non-living systems of the earth in order to maintain their sustainability for present and future, allowing development with equity'. Acceptance of this ethic involves responsibility, freedom, justice, truthfulness, sensitivity and awareness; and leads to a series of obligations, some of which are difficult for politicians to accept (impact assessment, monitoring and publication of results, full accounting, easing of technological transfer, polluter pays, transnational recompensation, etc).

The Code is, of course, not a Christian document, but the three elements of the ethic (stewardship, sustainability, and quality of life produced by development with equity) are scriptural notions, and the Code can be regarded as a statement of biblical principles. God cares for the whole world; not a sparrow dies without him knowing; he causes the rain to fall on the just and the unjust alike. I believe the preparation of the Code was as religious an activity as almost any we carry out in the name of the church. Just as God calls scientists as well as pastors, so he abhors us erecting barriers between different parts of our life. The evolution–creation debates have made us face the fact that God is both immanent and transcendent; the environmental debate has forced us to recognise anew that we are all stewards—not merely of time, money or talents, but of all the resources of God's creation. The challenge that Christians who are scientists should be presenting to the church and the world alike is to recognise the greatness of the Lord—Creator, Redeemer and Sustainer.

Humpty Dumpty

We often speak of someone's world crashing in pieces or their 'life falling apart', with the implication that 'all the king's men couldn't put it together again'. I suppose my future appeared like that when my father died. My testimony from that time and on many subsequent occasions has been of the wholeness which the Lord gives. This should not be surprising; the Greek work *soteria* which we translate as 'salvation' literally means 'wholeness'. Such wholeness (or 'healing') should pervade all parts of our life, uniting body, mind and soul. It links evolution and creation, law and miracle, environmental care and stewardship.

Charles Darwin was buried in Westminster Abbey (after some jiggery-pokery by T.H. Huxley and Francis Galton, who wanted to make a political point about science triumphing over superstition). An anthem was composed specially for the funeral by Frederick Bridge, the abbey organist, based on Proverbs 3:13: 'Blessed is the man who has found wisdom, he who has acquired understanding'. I don't know whether Darwin actually achieved understanding but I am utterly persuaded that the inclusive wisdom which begins with the fear and wonder of God and which was granted to Solomon (1 Kings 3:9) is necessary and, through God's Spirit, available to all of us who are open to it.

If I draw one lesson from my experiences as a scientist and a Christian, it is that compartmentalisation of life, thought or worship is damaging and potentially dangerous. The gospel involves reconciliation between body and spirit, and sacred and secular, as well as between God and humankind. In my own research, I have repeatedly had to straddle the boundaries between traditional disciplines—ranging between ecology, genetics, geography, pathology, history, physiology, behaviour and others. In my spiritual life, I have similarly tried to worship my God in laboratory, field and church alike—not as a vague influence, but as a personal Lord, Saviour, Guide, Comforter.

One of the few poems I have managed to learn since leaving school is a sonnet by Robert Rendall, an Orkney draper and naturalist, and a devoted member of his local Brethren Assembly. It is perhaps especially real to me because I have been involved in many scientific studies in Rendall's native islands. It is not an overtly Christian poem, but it incorporates the wholeness and balance of attitude which is the fruit of life in Christ.

> Scant are the few green acres I till,
> But arched above them spreads the boundless sky,
> Ripening their crops; and round them lie
> Long miles of moorland hill.
>
> Beyond the cliff-top glimmers in the sun
> The far horizon's bright infinity;
> And I can gaze across the sea
> When my day's work is done.
>
> The solitudes of land and sea assuage
> My quenchless thirst for freedom unconfined;
> With independent heart and mind
> Hold I my heritage.

Of course, we are called to speak of Christ and his saving grace whenever possible, but it must be in the context of a life and attitude which demonstrates the saving ('making whole') and transforming work which he has and is doing in individuals and communities alike. Science and faith have different methodologies, but they are complementary, not contradictory; a faith without reason is as stultifying as a reason without faith.

Notes

[1] I put the word in inverted commas. All those who believe in a Creator God are creationists, whether they believe God made the world more or less instantaneously, or through the evolutionary process. It is just as real for an evolutionist to affirm 'I believe in God, Maker of heaven and earth', as it is for a literal six-day 'creationist'.

[2] P.G.H. Clarke, *Nature,* vol 311 (1984): p 502.

[3] *Nature* vol 322 (1986): pp 321–322. My title for the reply was 'Miracles: scepticism, credulity or reality?' The Editor changed it to 'What to believe about miracles'. It was reprinted as an appendix to my book, *God and Evolution* (Hodder & Stoughton, 1988), and also (in a slightly changed form) in a book edited by Andrew Walker, *Different Gospels* (Hodder & Stoughton, 1988).

[4] William Kruksal, 'Miracles and statistics: the causal assumption of independence', *Journal of the American Statistical Association,* vol 83 (1988): pp 929–940.

16

Science and Christian Faith Today

Donald MacKay – Physicist and brain scientist

Professor Donald M. MacKay, BSc, PhD, DSc, F Inst Phys, FKC.
Born 1922, died 1987. Educated Wick High School, St Andrew's University and King's College, London.
Professor of Communication, University of Keele, 1960–82.
Foreign Member, Royal Netherlands Academy of Arts and Science, 1983.
Herman von Helmholtz Prize for Distinguished Research in the Cognitive Neurosciences, 1985.
Edington Lecturer, University of Cambridge, 1967.
Foerster Lecturer, University of California, Berkeley, 1973.
Gifford Lecturer, University of Glasgow, 1986.

A century ago it looked to many people as if science and Christian faith were heading for a fight to the death. Today the echoes of the conflict have almost died away. Is this 'peace with honour', or is it a dishonourable truce? I believe the dispute deserved to die, because it was not really between science and Christianity at all but between mistaken views of each; and I would maintain that the true scientific spirit in fact expresses something which is a necessary ingredient of a truly Christian faith. Faith is not credulity; like scientific belief, it entails trust based on experience and on reliable testimony. It differs from scientific belief not in its standard of truth but in its mode of origin.

Both Christians and scientists have learned something since the debates of the last century. Christians have come to realise that true reverence for the Bible requires a positive effort to avoid misinterpreting it; and that scientific discoveries may sometimes be God's way of warning us off a too literal approach. Scientists have been taught by science itself to distinguish more carefully between fact and interpretation, and have recovered some of their professional humility.

It would be mistaken, however, to use any *technical* changes in science (eg, physical indeterminacy) as an argument for Christian faith. The Bible represents God as 'upholding' the whole going universe—not merely the physically puzzling bits. While, to our finite minds, the idea of 'upholding' or 'holding in being' can convey only a hint of the truth, it serves at least to guard us against the image of a mechanic tending a machine.

It would be equally fallacious to argue from the present regularities that miraculous events, such as the resurrection of Christ, were 'scientifically impossible'. Just as a scene on a television screen, however 'regular' it seems, could be unimaginably changed by merely turning a switch, so God's world is open to change at his will. The big difference is that no change in God's world could ever be capricious. God's actions may sometimes be astonishing to *us*; but they can never be inconsistent with *his* unchanging purposes. This is what distinguishes miracle (in the biblical sense) from mere magic. It is here, indeed, that I see the deepest harmony between Christian faith and the scientific attitude. The best basis for our scientific expectations is the rationality and faithfulness of the God who holds our world in being.

The basic issue

Three centuries ago, the founders of the Royal Society saw nothing incongruous in dedicating their scientific work 'to the glory of God'.

Two centuries ago, the new discoveries of science were being eagerly harnessed to 'arguments from design' intended to support the Christian faith.

A century later, the climate of thought had changed; theologians and scientists were eyeing one another with mutual distrust, and before long men were speaking and writing as though science and Christianity were in for a fight to the death.

Today, the echoes of the great nineteenth-century conflict have almost died away, and theologians and scientists once more pursue their callings side by side in peace.

The true scientific spirit expresses something which is not only a possible but a necessary ingredient of a fully Christian faith. Christian faith is not credulity; like scientific belief, in one respect at least, it is *trust based on experience and on testimony judged reliable*. (This is not of course meant as a complete *definition* of faith!)

As everyone knows, the ostensible cause of battle in the past century was the Darwinian theory of evolution; but I have no qualifications to discuss the technicalities then in dispute, and in any case I believe that the basic dispute concerned a much more general question, which evolutionary biology just happened to raise in an acute form.

The Christian God is declared throughout the Bible to be a God of *action*. He not only is; he *does*. Science, however, is concerned to account for everything that happens in terms of other happenings ('causes') in the physical world. The chain-mesh of cause-and-effect is far from complete; but missing links are continually being found, and most nineteenth-century scientists saw no obstacle to its eventual completion.

What then of the God of action? This was the real

question underlying the great debate. Did science, in its ever-filling picture, leave any room for God to act? To many scientists the idea of God seemed obviously a mere stopgap for want of scientific knowledge of what they would call the 'real causes' of events. Some of the ablest theologians encouraged this belief by desperately searching for weakness in the scientific theories they regarded as competitive—performing in the process a valuable service to science, but fated to be squeezed from one untenable position to another under the pressure of accumulating fact. The very momentum of their retreat contributed to the general impression that the Christian faith was no longer credible for an honest and well-informed Victorian.

Changes—relevant and otherwise

What has happened between then and now to account for the different outlook today? Changes there have been in plenty. First, and most spectacular, has come the complete revision of our scientific notion of the physical world, culminating in Heisenberg's famous *Principle of Uncertainty*. According to this, the 'elementary particles' of the universe (electrons and the like) are fundamentally unpredictable in their motions. Either the speed or the position of an electron may be determined as exactly as we please—but not both exactly at the same time. At any one time we have to make a compromise, accepting less precision in the one specification if we demand more in the other. The average behaviour of large enough numbers of particles, like the average numbers of births or deaths in a large community, can, of course, be predicted more accurately, so that the dynamics of objects as large as billiard balls or planets are unaffected; but the Victorian dream of a 'clockwork universe' of fully-predictable processes has been shattered.

I have begun with this particular change, not because I think it is crucial to the Christian position, but because I think it is not; and I fear that some—though by no means all—apologists have been tempted to make more of it than they should. Heisenberg's principle does establish a certain kind of incompleteness in the scientific picture which we are far from understanding; but the 'gaps' it indicates are not at all of the kind for which nineteenth-century theologians were looking; and in any case I hope to show that a fully biblical doctrine of God's activity is made logically neither more nor less credible by such developments.

The second big change—in part a consequence of the first—is in the *mood* of scientists. By contrast with the jaunty confidence of last century, it could, I think, be fairly described as 'chastened'. Particularly in the physical sciences, cocksure dogmatism has given place to a much more cautious and tentative way of presenting conclusions. Arrogant postures may occasionally be struck by a few exponents of the newer sciences, such as molecular biology and anthropology; but these attitudes are widely deplored by fellow scientists as atypical. It is sometimes said that the bankruptcy of classical physics, revealed by the discoveries of atomic phenomena, discredited Victorian materialism. For its logical implications I believe this makes too strong a claim; but at the psychological level I think it is profoundly true. These discoveries, from within science itself, have done much to recall us in science to a proper professional humility.

There have been changes, too, on the other side. I am not thinking now of the various attempts to compromise, in the name of 'modernism', by abandoning unpalatable biblical doctrines and biblical authority. I believe such a compromise to be neither necessary, nor, in the long run, self-consistent. The lesson that all Christians have learned, however, is that what may seem the 'obvious' way to interpret biblical material is not always the most reverent; that true reverence for the Bible requires a positive effort to avoid misinterpreting it. Sometimes it may even be scientific observations that God uses to warn us when we are pressing a literal scientific interpretation on a non-scientific idiom (as when Copernican astronomy came up against the official geocentric interpretation of passages such as Psalm 104:5). It has never been doubted by orthodox Christians that the same God was the Author of true discoveries in the book of nature as well as in the book of Scripture. But instead of arguing, as some did a hundred years ago, that this rendered scientific enquiry superfluous on matters dealt with in Scripture, Christians today are more alive both to the dangers of trying to use Scripture for purposes which it is not intended to serve, and to their responsibility, in God's sight, for following up the full implications of the knowledge he gives in these other ways.

The second big change—or rather, reformation—on the Christian side, has been in the understanding of what is meant by God's activity in relation to our world. Like all true religious reformations, this has been marked by a revival of emphasis on what the Bible actually has to say, as opposed to what it was thought to say or expected to say. In forcing this re-examination of thought-models, the nineteenth-century conflict has been an undoubted blessing. The trouble was that both Christians and non-Christians at that time had slipped into thinking of God as a kind of *machine-tender*. Partly under the influence of deistic notions, and of such stock works of apologetic as Paley's *Evidences,* they were tacitly agreed in adopting a mental picture of the world as a great machine, with God (if he existed) supervising its workings from outside. Divine activity in the world (if any) would then be possible only if parts of the machine were open to non-mechanical influence. Hence the importance attached to 'gaps' in the chain-mesh of physical cause-and-effect, to enable God to intervene without wrenching a part of the (presumably perfect) machinery.

Undoubtedly, there are various biblical idioms which could be taken in isolation to justify this mental picture (eg, Gen 2:2; Ps 102:25); and indeed, for practical purposes, it embodies an important truth, that God's normal pattern for his world is regular and reliable as clockwork. No single image need be expected to do justice to all aspects of his relationship to the universe, and it may well be asked why such a time-honoured (if relatively recent) thought-model should be set aside. An image has had its day, however, when its power to illuminate is exceeded by its power to mislead; and in our time this would seem to be abundantly true of the picture of God as a machine-tender. It is not that it cannot be stretched *ad hoc* to fit the biblical data it purports to embody, but rather that the *expectations* it evokes are radically out of key with much of what the Bible has to say about God's activity. Instead of finding a ready place within its framework, concepts such as creation or miracle appear as disconcerting 'difficulties', felt by non-Christians at least to be vaguely incoherent with the rest of the picture they are offered. Worst of all, the whole facet of biblical teaching that deals with God as immanent in the events of nature is made to seem quite unintelligible.

For when we look at it more closely, the Bible as a whole represents God in far too intimate and active a relationship to daily events to be represented in these mechanical terms. He does not come in only at the beginning of time to 'wind up the works'; he continually 'upholds all things by the word of his power' (Heb 1:3). 'In him [ie, Christ] all things hold together' (Col 1:17). Here is an idea radically different from that of tending or interfering with a machine. It is not only the physically inexplicable happenings (if any), but the whole going concern that the Bible associates with the constant activity of God. God is the primary agent in feeding the ravens, or clothing the lilies (Lk 12:22–28); it is he who is active in the 'natural' processes of rainfall and of growth; and even wicked men depend on him for their existence (Mt 5:45) and serve his purposes (Acts 2:23). The whole multi-patterned drama of our universe is declared to be continually 'held in being' and governed by him.

Divine upholding

What sense can we make of this unfamiliar idea of 'holding in being'? Obviously it describes a mystery that we need not expect to understand at all fully; yet unless we can make something of it we cannot come to grips with its relation to our scientific and everyday ways of thinking about the world, which is our present concern.

To start with a negative, it is clearly meant to warn us against precisely the error we have been discussing, of reducing God to the status of a machine-tender. While insisting on the genuine distinction between God and his creation, the Bible throughout regards his activity as essential to, and visible in, all its continuing processes. Can we find a mental image that will do more justice to this relationship? We need not expect to invent a perfect analogy; and if I venture to suggest a possible thought-model it is only because I have found that it helps to tie together a range of biblical and scientific ideas somewhat wider than those covered by the earlier image, though still inevitably limited.

An imaginative artist brings into being a world of his own invention. He does it normally by laying down patches of paint on canvas, in a certain spatial order (or disorder!). The *order* which he gives the paint determines the *form* of the world he invents. Imagine now an artist able to bring his world into being, not by laying down paint on canvas, but by producing an extremely rapid succession of sparks of light on the screen of a television tube. (This is in fact the way in which a normal television picture is held in being.) The world he invents is now not static but dynamic, able to change and evolve at his will. Both its form and its laws of change (if any) depend on the way in which he orders the sparks of light in space and time. With one sequence he produces a calm landscape with quietly rolling clouds; with another, we are looking at a vigorous cricket match on a village green. The scene is steady and unchanging just for as long as he wills it so; but if he were to cease his activity, his invented world would not become chaotic; it would simply cease to be.

I do not in fact know anyone with sufficient dexterity to perform such feats at the required speed; but that is beside the point. I have sketched our hypothetical artist at work because I find this process quite a helpful illustration of some of the ways in which the Bible talks about God's activity in physical events.

Suppose, for example, that we are watching a cricket match 'brought into being' and 'held in being' by such an artist. We see the ball hit the wicket and the stumps go flying. The 'cause' of the motion of the stumps, in the ordinary sense, is the impact of the ball. Indeed, for any happening in and of the invented scene, we would normally look for—and expect to find—the 'cause' in some other happenings in and of that scene. Given a sufficiently long and self-consistent sample, we might in fact imagine ourselves developing a complete predictive *science* of the cricket world displayed before us, abstracting 'laws of motion' sufficient to explain satisfactorily (in a scientific sense) every happening we witness—so long as the artist keeps to the same regular principles in maintaining the cricket scene in being.

Suppose, however, that someone suggests that our scientific explanation of these happenings is 'not the only one', and that all our experience of them owes its existence to the continuing stability of the will of the artist who shapes and 'holds in being' the whole going concern. However odd this may sound at first, it is obvious that in fact he is not advancing a *rival* explanation to the one we have discovered in our 'science' of the cricket field; he has no need to cast doubt on ours in order to make room for his own, since the two are not explanations *in the same sense*. They are answers to different questions, and both may, in fact, be entirely valid.

The parallel I think is clear as far as it goes. The God in

whom the Bible invites belief is no 'cosmic mechanic'. Rather is he the Cosmic Artist, the creative Upholder, without whose continual activity there would be not even chaos, but just nothing. What we call physical laws are expressions of the regularity that we find in the pattern of created events that we study as the physical world. Physically, they express the nature of the entities 'held in being' in the pattern. Theologically, they express the stability of the great Artist's creative will. Explanations in terms of scientific laws and in terms of divine activity are thus not rival answers to the same question; yet they are not talking about different things. They are (or at any rate purport to be) complementary accounts of different aspects of the same happening, which in its full nature cannot be adequately described by either alone.

Before we turn to work out some of these implications in more detail, it may be well to make clear what is *not* implied by our illustration in this inadequate form. The human artist's invented world is unreal; but what God does is the only ultimate reality there is. The human artist's world is presented to us on a screen, of which we are merely powerless spectators. In God's world, however, we are part of the scene, brought into being as active participants as well as observers. Nor are we mere puppets. We contribute by our own decisions and actions to the total drama, and God holds us responsible for the part we play, even while our existence in it is wholly dependent upon him.

In these and doubtless other respects, then, the illustration is deficient and could be misleading in its turn; but while some of the deficiencies can, I think, be remedied, there is no need for our present purpose to complicate the thought-model. Its function is not (heaven forbid!) to explain the mystery of God's activity, but only to bring out some of the features of the biblical idea of it which seem to have been neglected in disputes where God was presumed to be a 'machine-tender'.

Prior to an enquiry into the truth or falsehood of the Bible's claim, there is a real need in our day to get clearer in mind what is, and what is· not, being claimed. If the biblical notion of 'holding in being' is at all akin to that which we have been considering, then the whole relation-ship between scientific and biblical analysis of 'causation' has to be reappraised. To argue hotly, for example, as some of our fathers did, whether something 'came about by natural causes *or* required an act of God', is simply not to take seriously the depth and range of the doctrine the Bible is asking us to consider. To invoke 'blind chance' as if it were an *alternative* to the action of God in creating us, as Professor Jacques Monod does in his book *Chance and Necessity,* similarly misconceives the Christian doctrine of creation and providence. For what in science we term 'chance events' are recognised in biblical theism as no more and no less dependent upon the sovereign creative power of God than the most law-abiding and predictable of happenings (Prov 16:33). It may be fair enough to express personal hostility to this doctrine; but it is theologically inept to pretend that science as such has any quarrel with it. The trouble here (to quote J.B. Phillips) is that our ideas of God have not been too big, but too small. Admittedly, the revision of our conception of 'reality' which the Bible calls for is far-reaching; but it is half-measures here that in the recent past have proved theologically disastrous. In the remainder of this paper I hope to bring out, with the help of a few key illustrations, the remarkable harmony of scientific and Christian belief which reappears when the nineteenth-century misunderstanding is replaced by a more thorough-going biblical emphasis.

Origins

Our first example may appropriately be the classical ques-tion of origins. As soon as we absorb the force of the biblical doctrine of God, it becomes clear that there is not just one question of origins, but two.

To enquire into the 'origin' of the cricket match on our artist's screen, for example, may be to ask *either* about the earlier pattern of happenings in the world of the cricket field that must presumably have led up to the scene we are now witnessing, *or* about the artist's originative activity, without which there would be no happenings at all. The first kind of 'origin' we could infer in principle from scientific or commonsense observation of the happenings in the scene, the state of the scoreboard, and so forth, extrapolating backwards from as many clues as we could pick up. The second, however, we should never expect to determine in this way. It is, of course, concerned in a sense with the past; but it is concerned to account for the past (and the present) of the picture as a whole—as a phenomenon so to speak—rather than with a unique moment in it. Only if the created scene contained some clues relating to the artist who is shaping and holding it in being could his existence, and the origin of the scene in this sense, even be discussed within *its* own framework. If it were so discussed, the appropriate term for it would certainly be the biblical 'ex nihilo'.

In relation to our own world as God's creation, much debate in the past seems to have arisen from a confusion of these two questions of origin. Cosmology, on the one hand, is concerned to extrapolate backwards in time on the presumption of continuity, and to picture the initial situation (if any) to which the present state of affairs would form a 'natural' sequel. The Bible, on the other hand, claims to be the clue to the origin of the world in our second, quite different, sense; not to its origin in time, but to its origin in eternity. Its basic concern is to reveal the nature and purposes of the Giver of the pattern we encounter as the physical world.

Even the first chapter of Genesis, despite its narrative form, makes clear, I think, that scientific 'history' is not what it means to convey. Its pictures—especially if their details are studied in contrast to pagan myths of the time—teach something quite other, and deeper, than cosmology. They tell us 'who' and 'why', and the metaphysical order of priorities, rather than 'how' in the physicist's sense. It may be worth while to substantiate this point in some detail, for too many people, including some 'modernist' Christians, have been apt to speak of Genesis 1 as a 'primitive attempt' by its writer to guess at what science has now revealed. In point of fact, the very structure of the Genesis narrative should have precluded this interpretation, since the story ends its creative period of six 'days' with a complete, going universe, in which the writer clearly intended us to picture trees and animals, for example, more than six days old. Logically, then, the Genesis narrative resembles an account of the way in which an artist brings his scene into being; it leaves entirely *open* the field of investigation we call 'cosmological origins', which must be determined by empirical examination of the scene—God's universe as created. Nor is there any suggestion that the past so determined—still less the present—is only 'apparent' or 'illusory': it is *the only past there is,* in the sense that science gives to the term. As Augustine put it long ago, God's creation is not *in tempore* but *cum tempore*: our scientific scale of time, extending backwards into the inferable past, is one of the intrinsic properties of the created order, and the biblical notion of creation as imaged in Genesis 1 is grossly distorted and diminished if it is restricted to a happening locatable at a point on that timescale, as if this were the point behind which scientific extrapolation must be impossible. The relationship of the divine Creator to our world is still more comprehensive, and the Bible's claim is in fact a bolder one. To draw a crude metaphor from our earlier illustration, Genesis 1, read at its face value, appears to narrate not just the inferable past of the 'cricket match', but rather the artist's decisions as to the kind of match it should be. I do not pretend that this is at all a clear notion, except insofar as our own experience of 'creative activity', eg, in writing, may afford some dim analogy.[1] But I see no reason to make any more complicated claim for the narrative such as (by reading the 'days' as aeons of geological time) that it represents a disguised version of the past that the scientist can discover. The intention of such speculations is often the excellent one of harmonising scientific discovery and inspired Scripture; our suggestion is only that the Scripture here *is not answering the same question,* so that to try to make it do so is to do it violence. It needs to be defended not against 'science' but against well-meaning (or any other) attempts to make it into 'science'.

By the same token, it would seem that any attempt to find support for the Christian doctrine of creation in 'explosive' theories of cosmology (which trace things back to a 'primeval atom') and to oppose the 'steady state' theories of Hoyle and others on *religious* grounds, would be misguided. The cosmological past of God's world is presumably 'written into' its present structure by him, and he will expect us to look for it there with unprejudiced eyes, since we cannot specify in advance which kind he should have 'written'. The most we can say *a priori* is that nothing can happen or have happened in our world that is inconsistent with the character of its Author.[2] Steady-state cosmologies may have some objections to face on scientific grounds, but they would seem to have none *a priori* in the Christian doctrine of creation.[3]

My contention then is not that the narrative here should be read literally (since I do not know what it could mean if one tried to), but that it should be read for what it is—a revelation of the *metaphysical* origins of our world—and not as either a 'primitive guess' or an inspired cryptogram on the *scientific* question of the cosmological past. Only in this way can we clear our minds for the depths of meaning that in faith we believe it to hold, for us just as much as for our less 'scientific' forebears.

Obviously this leaves a problem of identifying the

transition in the biblical record from the 'divine history' of origins, to the 'natural history' of our created order. I have no intention of suggesting a clear-cut solution, for I do not believe that the transition itself is clear-cut. I want only to contend for the reality and necessity of the distinction.

What has been said about physical origins would seem to apply equally to questions of the origin of man's sense of moral values. Conflict can surely arise here only if our two questions of origin are confused. On the one hand there is the technical scientific question of the inferable past history of man's moral ideas; on the other, the theological question of their divine givenness or otherwise. Data are so sparse that present 'evolutionary' answers to the first question may be far wrong; but if they are wrong, there would seem to be no biblical reason to doubt that there is *some* answer to it in terms of mechanism which is right. I have already suggested that on closer examination the narrative in Genesis is not logically framed to supply us with an answer of this sort; its concern is within the second question. From the biblical viewpoint, to argue whether a sense of values developed naturally or was divinely given is to accept a false antithesis. To invoke 'natural processes' is not to escape from divine activity, but only to make hypotheses about its regularity; and the historical development of a perceptual mechanism, whether in the single individual or in the race, is quite a different matter from the origin and validity of what is perceived. (For example, we cannot settle the validity of our ideas in geometry by discussing the embryological origin of the brain!)

Undoubtedly there have been some anti-Christian biologists who thought—and claimed—otherwise; but the biblical answer to such men would seem to be to question, not their science (unless for scientific reasons!), but their confounding of the metaphysical origin of ethics with the physical or psychological origin of man's 'ethical mechanisms'. Space does not allow a full discussion of the biblical doctrine of man; but inasmuch as the Bible regards man as a psychophysical unity, it implies that *some* physical account of the development of each of his faculties in their mechanical aspects is necessarily required, as the complement to the revealed facts of their divine origin. Even complete continuity of physical development would not, of course, preclude discontinuity of spiritual nature between man and other animals. To use a simply analogy, the proportion of gas to air in a burner may be increased continuously until the mixture suddenly sustains a flame. But when this happens we have a qualitatively new entity, with a dynamics of its own, and with nothing to correspond to it in the earlier stages. Similarly, even in a continuous theory of human evolution (if anyone wants to speculate along these lines) one would have to reckon with the likelihood that the growth of a truly 'human' pattern of organisation, in the brain of the first true man, would be a self-catalysing process, raising him at one bound to a qualitatively new spiritual capacity inconceivable to his predecessors. My aim is not to recommend such speculations, but simply to emphasise the appropriateness of 'reverent agnosticism', here as elsewhere, admitting our ignorance when conclusive evidence is not supplied either by revelation or observation.

Natural laws

A second example of the biblical approach illustrated here concerns the notion of 'natural law'. As long as the world is thought of as a kind of machine, natural laws are bound to have something of the character of invisible cogwheels and levers. As soon as we move to the more dynamic thought-model illustrated by our artist and his screen, however, the notion of law takes on quite a new aspect.

In the cricket field on the screen it is possible to discover numerous examples of orderly behaviour that could be subsumed under general 'laws'. Quite possibly, as already mentioned, we might develop a successful deterministic *science* of the behaviour we are watching. As long—but only as long—as the artist's activity maintains the required regularities, our predictions should succeed. If his pattern were to change, or to fluctuate irregularly, our predictions might be upset, to a greater or lesser degree. But—and this is the point—the presence of such unpredictable happenings is not in the least *essential* to our belief that the whole scene of activity is held in being by the artist. In particular, whether the 'natural laws' we discover in the scene are deterministic or indeterministic (ie, statistical) *makes no difference* to our belief that it has a Creator who is in control of it. This belief does not rest on that kind of evidence.

Perhaps you see now why I insisted earlier that it is a mistake to harness Heisenberg's principle to Christian apologetic. For here, too, the question whether physical laws are deterministic or indeterministic in the scientific sense is irrelevant to the Bible's claim that they betoken the continuance of God's maintaining 'programme'. Thus whereas some have argued that only an indeterministic physics leaves *room* for God to act in our world, while others, like Monod, see the element of randomness as *eliminating* the possibility of divine control, biblical theism, if I understand it correctly, accepts neither of these mutually cancelling arguments. For the Christian, as we have noted, the events we classify scientifically as 'chance' are as much divinely given as any others; and natural law is primarily an expression of God's faithfulness in giving a succession of experience that is coherent and predictable. 'While the earth remains, seedtime and harvest, cold and heat, summer and winter, day and night shall not cease' (Gen 8:22). Thus the common saying that God can 'use' natural means to achieve his ends, while undoubtedly true in its intended sense, suggests by its wording quite the wrong relationship of God to natural law. It would seem more correct to say that God sometimes achieves his ends *in 'natural' ways* (ie, in ways that do not upset precedent from a scientific point of view). God is not like a man, *using* his laws as tools that would exist independently of him; it is he who brings into being and holds in being the activities, whether scientifically 'lawful' or otherwise, that we may recognise to be serving his ends.

Once his programme has reached its final consummation, moreover, we are told that the whole of the present world shall be 'rolled together like a scroll', to give place to something unimaginably better (Is 34:4; 2 Pet 3:13).

Miracle

Discussion of natural law leads directly to the problem of miracle. The old objection to miracles was that they involved God in tampering with his own mechanism—an intervention which was pronounced either scientifically impossible or theologically improper, according to taste. Against the full biblical doctrine of the natural world, however, the objection loses any force it had. In the first place, while the biblical concept of natural law, as we have seen, supplies the highest reasons for normally relying on our scientific expectations, it renders meaningless any notion of 'scientific impossibility' where God is concerned. Just as even an ordinary television picture may be unimaginably altered at the turn of a switch, so God's world is entirely open to change at his will.

The last phrase, however, which might seem a gateway to all irrationality, embodies, of course, the most vitally important safeguard. Since the stability of God's will is declared to be the origin and foundation and standard of all rationality, no change that he sees fit to make in his 'programme' could ever be *capricious*. He it is who makes and maintains the whole of his creation 'a cosmos, not a chaos'. Some of his actions at special turning-points in history may have been astonishing to us, and his sovereign

will does not abide our question; but we are never encouraged to regard them as irrational. This forms a crucial
distinction in principle between biblical miracle and magic.

The Bible always presents a miracle, however physically
surprising, as the *self-consistent* expression, at that particular point in history, of God's unchanging faithfulness to the
purpose (however inscrutable) for which he has brought
the whole pattern of events into being. Even of the central
miracle of Christ's resurrection, Peter says that it was
impossible that death should hold him (Acts 2:24). Appropriateness and rationality (as seen from the standpoint
of eternity, though not necessarily manifest to us), are
declared to be of the essence of the biblical concept of
miracle. The Christian has no warrant to believe in a God
of caprice.

It follows from all this that a biblical miracle is made
neither more nor less credible by attempts (however well-
intentioned) to find a 'natural' process to account for its
physical manifestations. What makes a miracle is not
primarily its violation of scientific expectations (though this
might be one result), but rather its function as an outstanding sign of God's power and purpose in the situation to
which it comes. In some cases this might require nothing
that need have shocked a scientist as such, the significance
being in the timing rather than the manner of events; in
others, if the record is to be read at its face value, it seems
hard to deny that the normal *pattern* of events was radically
altered. In every case it is clear that the event could not
have fulfilled its communicative purpose unless it had been
out of the ordinary in some sense for those concerned. My
point is simply that the God of biblical doctrine would have
no difficulty in bringing about the one kind of event any
more than the other; but that the biblical doctrine nevertheless provides a more stable, rather than a less stable,
foundation for our normal scientific expectations, in the
stability of the will of a God who is always faithful.

The ground of faith

All I have said thus far is in one sense merely permissive. I have shown, I hope, that the biblical doctrine of divine activity is not only compatible with our scientific knowledge, but also positively encouraging to the attitude towards natural events that we call scientific. At most, however, all such demonstrations can make Christianity only plausible. They are bound to leave us still with the question whether it is true, and how we can be convinced that it is.

Before concluding, then, we must return briefly to the point made at the start: that faith, like scientific belief, is a kind of trust that is based on personal experience as well as on testimony judged reliable. Christian faith is not just a body of second-hand beliefs, however self-consistent—not even if acquired from the Bible itself. Its essence is an active, day-to-day relationship of personal dependence on and obedience to the Giver of our daily round as he has revealed himself and his will in Christ and Scripture, in fellowship with other Christians—a relationship which both illuminates, and is illuminated by, the doctrines from which it is inseparable.

Neither personal experience divorced from biblical doctrine, nor intellectual acceptance of doctrine divorced from experience and practice, can sustain faith in the biblical sense. It is the day-to-day personal confirmation that God is as good as his word given in the Bible, together with the intellectual outworking of the implications of God's acts and purposes revealed there, that combine and interact cumulatively to grip the heart and mind and will with the authoritative conviction we refer to as faith.

I should perhaps emphasise that by 'experience' here I am not referring to the esoteric feelings of the mystic, which are often taken as the paradigm of 'the religious experience'. I mean rather something which at the psychological level may be quite prosaic and ordinary, though different from sensory experience of the external world:

namely, the whole realm of our moral experience, at the level of willing and choosing. 'Whoever is willing to do the will of my Father,' said Jesus, 'shall come to know of my teaching whether it is from God' (Jn 7:17). To know the authoritative grip of God's will on one's conscience need involve no abnormal psychological phenomena; but it is the kind of experience that gives empirical content to otherwise theoretical talk of a personal relationship with him. It is not, of course, a matter of uncritically renaming in pious terms all that everyone experiences at this level. This would be mere superstition, akin to the reading of 'messages' in an undisciplined sequence of words from a dictionary. In Christian doctrine God's promise to make himself known to us in personal experience is conditional on our approaching him by the way and in the spirit that the Bible indicates—ready for any consequence of discovering and following the purpose for which he has brought us and our whole world into being. This is no 'nodding acquaintance', for there are deep things to be settled between each of us and God. By nature we prefer purposes of our own quite at variance with his; and for anyone who takes God at his word such unfamiliar concepts as repentance, atonement, forgiveness and grace turn out to have a definite operational significance that may hurt even as it heals.

But my purpose now is not to expound the Christian gospel. It has rather been to bring out something of what I meant by saying at the beginning that faith differs from scientific belief, not in its standards of truth but in its mode of origin. Esential checks against undisciplined subjectivism exist in the biblical revelation itself and in the testimony of fellow Christians past and present; hence in part the importance that has always been attached to intelligent study of the Bible, and to the fellowship of Christians in the church. It is only within this objective framework that the Christian's experience in stumbling obedience can validly grow into the astonished conviction that his faith is the sober truth.

Conclusion

We are emerging from a period of confused conflict during which the biblical doctrine of divine activity seems to have become largely distorted or forgotten. It is in this doctrine, untrimmed by any concessions to the spirit of our age, that I see the basis of the deepest harmony between Christian faith and the scientific attitude. There could be no better basis for our scientific expectations than the rationality and faithfulness of the One who holds in being the stuff and pattern of our world.

Notes

[1] For a brilliant essay on this theme see Dorothy Sayers' *The Mind of the Maker*.

[2] This does not of course imply that we can deduce the character of its Author solely from what *we* are able to see in his world. The doctrine of the Fall indicates that the whole present 'programme' as we encounter it bears the marks of our chosen relationship of rebelliousness towards its Giver, so that apart from Christ's revelation of God's 'eternal purpose' we could go hopelessly astray as to his nature.

[3] In justice it should be said that the essence of this point seems to have been appreciated by the much-ridiculed Philip Henry Gosse, FRS, who is best remembered for suggesting that God created the rocks with the fossils *in situ*. Certainly Gosse seems to have given his contemporaries the impression that 'the creation' was a datable event a few thousand years ago on our timescale; and in this I have no wish to defend him. But, with all his faults, I think he showed more insight into the logic of the Genesis narrative than opponents such as Charles Kingsley, who held that on Gosse's theory the Creator had perpetrated a deliberate falsehood by creating rocks complete with fossils. For whatever the peculiarities of Gosse's view, the point apparently missed by Kingsley is that *some* kind of inferable past is inevitably implicit in any going system, whether with fossils or without, so that to speak of 'falsehood' here is to

suggest a nonexistent option. Creation in the biblical sense is the 'willing into reality' of the *whole* of our space-time; future, present and past. If the Creator in the Genesis narrative were supposed to have made the rocks without fossils, this would not have helped, for nothing could have prevented the rocks from having *some* physically inferable past: their past would simply have been different, and moreover inconsistent with the rest of the created natural history. On Kingsley's argument, pressed to its logical conclusion, God ought not to have created any matter at all, since even molecules cannot help having some inferable past history!

Bibliography

This lists the more significant books referred to in preceding chapters. Some of them are only mentioned because the contributor criticises them. Recommended books (including some by writers in this book) are included in Further Reading.

Allen, C.J. *Two Million Miles of Rail Travel*. 1965.

Capra, F. *The Tao of Physics*. Oxford University Press: Oxford (reprinted by Fontana 1983).

Conservation and Development Programme for the UK. A response to the World Conservation Strategy. London: Kogan Page.

Coulson, C.A. *Science and Christian Belief*. Oxford University Press: London, 1955.

Darwin, C. *On the Origin of Species by Means of Natural Selection, or the Preservation of Favoured Races in the Struggle for Life*. John Murray: London, 1859.

Dawkins, R. *The Blind Watchmaker*, Longman: London, 1986 (reprinted by Penguin, 1986).

Gleick, J. *Chaos*. Heinemann: London, 1988 (reprinted in paperback by Sphere).

Gould, S.J. *Wonderful Life*. Hutchinson Radius: London, 1989.

Hawking, S. *A Brief History of Time*. Bantam: London, 1988.

Huxley, J.S. (ed). *The Humanist Frame*. George Allen & Unwin: London, 1961.

Lovelock, J.E. *The Ages of Gaia*. Oxford University Press: Oxford, 1988.

Medawar, P. *The Limits of Science*. Harper & Row: New York, 1984; and Oxford University Press: Oxford, 1984.

Monod, J. *Chance and Necessity*. Collins: London, 1972. (Originally published as *La Hasard et la necessite* by Editions du Seuil: Paris, 1970).

Moore, J.R. *The Post-Darwinian Controversies*. Cambridge University Press: Cambridge, 1979.

Morison, F. *Who Moved the Stone?* Faber: London, 1930.

Paley, W. *Natural Theology; or Evidences of the Existence and Attributes of the Deity Collected from the Appearances of Nature*. R. Faulder: London, 1802.

Penrose, R. *The Emperor's New Mind*. Oxford University Press: Oxford, 1989.

Russell, B. *Religion and Science*. Oxford University Press: Oxford, 1935.

Sargant, W. *Battle for the Mind*. Heinemann: London, 1957.

Simpson, P.C. *The Fact of Christ*. Hodder & Stoughton: London, 1900.

Teilhard de Chardin, P. *Phenomenon of Man*. Collins: London, 1959.

World Conservation Strategy. International Union for the Conservation of Nature and Natural Resources, in co-operation with the United Nations Environment Programme and the World Wildlife Fund. IUCN: Gland, Switzerland, 1980.

Further Reading

There are a large number of books on science and faith. The following books are intended to help readers delve further in the subject.

Barbour, I.G. *Issues in Science and Religion*. SCM: London, 1966.

Barker, M.G. *Starting Psychiatry*. Christian Medical Fellowship: London, 1971.

Berry, A.C. *The Rites of Life*. Hodder & Stoughton: London, 1987.

Berry, R.J. *God and Evolution*. Hodder & Stoughton: London, 1988.

Burke, D. (ed). *Where Christians Differ: Creation and Evolution*. IVP: Leicester, 1985.

Forster, R. and Marston, P. *Reason and Faith*. Monarch: Eastbourne, 1989.

Granberg-Michaelson, W. (ed). *Tending the Garden. Essays on the Gospel and the Earth*. Eerdmans: Grand Rapids, Michigan, 1987.

Hawthorne, J.N. *Windows of Science and Faith*. IVP: Leicester, 1987.

Helm, P. (ed). *Objective Knowledge*. IVP: Leicester, 1987.

Henry, C.F.H. (ed). *Horizons of Science*. Harper & Row: New York, 1978.

Hookyaas, R. *Religion and the Rise of Modern Science*. Scottish Academic Press: Edinburgh, 1972.

Houghton, J.T. *Does God Play Dice?* IVP: Leicester, 1988.

Hummel, C.E. *The Galileo Connection*. IVP: Downers Grove, Illinois, 1986.

Humphreys, C.J. *Creation and Evolution*. Oxford University Press: Oxford, 1985.

Jeeves, M.A. (ed). *Scientific Enterprise and Christian Faith*. Tyndale: London, 1969.

Jeeves, M.A. *Psychology and Christianity: the view both ways*. IVP: Leicester, 1976.

Jeeves, M.A. (ed). *Behavioural Sciences: a Christian Perspective*. IVP: Leicester, 1984. (Contains chapters by Donald MacKay, Sam Berry, Duncan Vere, Monty Barker, and others.)

Livingstone, D.N. *Darwin's Forgotten Defenders. The Encounter Between Evangelical Theology and Evolutionary Thought*. Eerdmans: Grand Rapids, Michigan; and Scottish Academic Press: Edinburgh.

MacKay, D.M. (ed). *Christianity in a Mechanistic University*. IVP: London. (Contains essays by Frank Rhodes, Donald MacKay, David Ingram, and Robert Boyd.)

MacKay, D.M. *The Clockwork Image*. IVP: Leicester, 1974.

MacKay, D.M. *Human Science and Human Dignity*. Hodder & Stoughton: London, 1979.

MacKay, D.M. *The Open Mind*. IVP: Leicester, 1988.

Peacock, R.E. *Foolish to be Wise*. Kingsway: Eastbourne, 1985.

Peacock, R.E. *A Brief History of Eternity*. Monarch: Eastbourne, 1989.

Ramm, B. *The Christian View of Science and Scripture*. Eerdmans: Grand Rapids, Michigan, 1954.

Russell, C.A. *Cross-currents. Interactions Between Science and Faith*. IVP: Leicester, 1985.

Scorer, C.G. and Wing, A. (eds). *Decision Making in Medicine*. Edward Arnold: London, 1979.

Stott, J.R.W. (ed). *Free to be Different*. Marshalls: Basingstoke, 1984. (Contains chapters by Malcolm Jeeves, Sam Berry and David Atkinson.)

Triton, A.N. *Whose World?* IVP: London, 1970.

Index